Table of contents

Introduction

1.1 More Wordpress and less coding

Worpdress is a Web builder which allows user to drag and drop for creating the landing page which is very fast and easy to learn. Wordpress is the best platform for the newbies who are more interested in growing online and starting their own blog. Wordpress can be used by any age range even if you are not from the technical background. The all you need is domain name, hosting and a blogging platform like wordpress where you can post your blog and get paid for the same. You might be living with a myth that you need to start coding for getting your business website or blog online. The fact is more than 27 billion sites are working on Wordpress including many brands like, the new York times, Sony music, the Walt Disney company, etc.

There are a lot of people in the society who have the skills to write and earn but are unaware of how to get started with Wordpress. You might be hearing with your friends and colleagues that to be a tech savvy you need to learn how to code and run. But as the myth is no more on rolling. The only concern will be that with 0 coding you will have limited features to perform but for your information, bloggers are earning more than 50,000 $ with only WordPress by writing their heart out.

You are very close to start work from home with the blog and you can easily get started by earning in 6 figures soon. The only way is to have the passion to learn and grow yourself in this pandemic so you will not have to worry about how to survive in bio wars if your jobs are layed off or you don't have a job. The dream to start your passion and kicking off 9 to 5 job can be only made true by loving WordPress and growing with this.

1.2 Difference between wordpress.com and wordpress.org

Everyone must have heard about the terms Wordpress.com and WordPress.org. We all know that these two terms are different from each other. Sometimes, a beginner gets confused with these two platforms and tends to select the wrong blogging platform. People use these platforms according to their needs, still, many are not aware of the differences between them.

WordPress.com: It is all about building your website without any need of hosting and domain names. In this method, one has to search for wordpress.com, and then you can quickly sign up and start creating your website.

WordPress.org: It is open-source software, which is an operating system for your website. To use it, one must have a hosting account that comes under a specific price. Both platforms have a similar working process.

1. **Price Comparison**

WordPress.com

Wordpress.com comes with many premium plans and features. You can easily create your website without any domain name or hosting account. One can use 3GB of disk space, and one has to co-operate the wordpress.com's advertisement throughout your site. The cheapest plan also provides the benefit of a free domain for one year.

WordPress.org

The wordpress.org platform is 100% free of cost. In case, if you want your website visible by the public, then, you must have to buy a hosting account and a domain name with a specific price.

2. **Setup Process**

WordPress.com

It is straightforward and convenient to use. Go to wordpress.com and click on the start of your website button. It will help us to understand each step, letting you know about your new website. One needs to enter the email and name of your website and select a creative design from a set of themes.

WordPress.org

The setup of wordpress.org is not so simple. However, in most cases, you don't visit wordPress.org to begin your website. Some of them start by selecting their choice of host and signing up there. While setting up a process at the host platform, you will get access to one or many methods of installing wordpress.org on your hosting account.

3. Themes

Wordpress.com

The selection of theme depends upon the wordPress.com features you select:

- The free plan provides more than 150 themes
- The premium plans provide more than 200 themes.

WordPress.org

In wordPress.org software, premium features, and the free plan provides thousands of themes. One can select more than 7500 themes from the leading directory at wordPress.org, and then you can install any other free one available on the web.

4. Customer support/help

Wordpress.com

The wordpress.com provides no support for the free plan. It only offers live support and email if you access the premium plans.

WordPress.org

No direct support from wordPress.org is possible. You can get help from only your web hosting provider. Some web hosts provide 24x7 supports.

 Note: We will be using Wordpress.org in this book. Choose the right hosting platform and you will get the support.

1.3 Wordpress over any other Web Builder

What is a Web Builder?

Suppose you want to do business, you have an excellent business plan to go with, a great team to move forward with your business plan. But in the end, you need Presence on the Web, the name of your business should be over the Internet and for that, you need a website. But neither you nor anyone in the team knows how to code a website. We all know coding is tricky, and not everyone's cup of tea. So the Solution for this is Website Builder.

A Website Builder is a utility or platform which allows you to make useful looking websites without or with knowing how to code. It works on drag and drops to add or customize the web page.

There are two types of Website Builders:

- Offline Website Builders
- Online Website Builders

For **Offline Website Builders**, you have to either buy or download the free versions, and you have to wait to upload your files to the web host until your website is complete on the local machine. The main down point of having offline website builders is you have to wait till your website gets ready locally, and you only can work on your local computer, which may not be that much mobile at some times, plus they are mostly platform[OS] dependent. Some of the Offline Website Builders are Adobe Dreamweaver, Adobe Muse CC, Mobirise, Webflow

While on the other hand, we have **Online Website Builders,** They only require an active Internet connection for working, and no software download requires like offline ones. So if they don't require any downloads, it means they are Platform[OS] Independent; you need an active internet connection and a device; yes, you can create a website from any corner of the world. Some of Online Website Builders are WordPress, Wix, Squarespace.

Any website builder consists of 3 essential steps to publish your website online:

- Just Select the Theme from the Theme Store (it might be free or paid), which suits your business idea.
- Edit or add the pre-present elements with drag and drop or click to add your own. Elements may be content, images, videos, social handles.
- Click on Publish Button

Why Wordpress over others?

There are many online Website Builders and Content management systems over the Internet, but most famous and most preferred from all of them is WordPress. WordPress solution can improve the user's online experience while answering a business's needs for website control, flexibility, and ease of use. Other reasons to use WordPress are:

1. **Wordpress is easy to use:** You don't need any expertise to work with WordPress, just little bit knowledge of drag and drop and lots of creativity. Its Dashboard service is enough for any layman to manage it.

2. **Wordpress is Free**: Unlike many other Paid CMS or Website Builders, WordPress is free to use. WordPress

is the best choice if you start any business and don't want to spend more on Websites and buying domains.

3. **Wordpress is Highly Customizable:** WordPress is highly customizable. You can set various attributes, including the privacy of content, pages to private and public, and you may save pages you're working on as Drafts and my schedule when they should be published. You can also categorize and tag your content.

4. **Wordpress is Seo Friednly:** WordPress also helps you grow in your SEO Ranks by suggesting that you add more keywords and take care of 70-90 percent of SEO of the Website.

5. **Wordpress is Interactive:** WordPress also has numerous features like auto-suggestion and auto-completion, plus you can add numerous plugins from the plugin store.

1.4 Participating in Wordpress Community

Even if you don't know to code, you can participate and join WordPress Community:

If you are serious about creating or running a website, then it is good to learn how to be a part of this community. And the whole WordPress community initiates to make the platform better because it's so significantly more than a secure site-building tool.The positive side is that if you know nothing about coding, the WordPress community welcomes everyone.

In this post, we will mention a few ways to start contributing to the WordPress community.**Is it worth becoming a WordPress Contributor?**

Yes, it's worth becoming a WordPress Contributor because there is a lot of advantage. You can grow your skills and helping to develop the platform. It's easier to build connections with clients and employers.

Its well said, "where there is a will, there is away."Even if you are new to the WordPress community with lots to learn or an experienced WordPress user with plenty to contribute, let's mention some of the top methods for adding to WordPress.

There are few ways to participate in the WordPress Community:

- **Teach development through testing**

In the WordPress community, development is one of the most favored and relevant fields. You don't have to be extraordinary to get started; all you want to know some necessary coding because developers are the ones who develop and refine the platform.

- **Write and edit documentation**

The WordPress community doesn't only want technical expertise, and they also needed many writers and editors to maintain running everything smoothly.

- **Build connections via community outreach**

The community outreach team works on a lot of different projects. If you want to get out there and interact with people, you will have the opportunity to participate in mentorship programs, volunteer at various events, and more.

WordPress community is also related to the events like word camp and meetup sessions:

The community outreach team works on the events and participate in programs. This team manages official events, mentorship programs, and volunteer at various events.

There are subordinates, many of them can speak multiple languages, and they present on six continents. The lead organizer is organizing each local meetup in the area, who regularly-scheduled events place simultaneously. Local meetup schedules can be different, but once every month, many groups meet.

On the other side, **WordCamps** are conferences that run by volunteers. The organizer doesn't make money from the events, and tickets are to help cover the cost.

How to start with Wordpress

2.1   Domain name and its impact

What is domain name?
Domain Name is the URL Address of your Website, which people type in the address bar, for example, at www.mybusiness.com. Domain Name is a mask to the IP Address of the machine on which your Website hosts. A Typical IP Address looks like this XXX.XXX.XXX.XXX. Just imagine how complicated it might be to remember those IP Addresses for every Website. That's why the concept of Domain Name came into existence. To not recognize the IP Addresses, but remember the domain names. Now, to access your favorite websites, you don't have to remember the long strings of IP Addresses, remember a secure domain name.

How does domain name work?
Before we know actually how Domain Name Works, first, we have to have the knowledge that what happens when we type the domain name of any website in your browser or search engine.
When you type any URL in your web browser, the request then goes to a global network of Domain Name Systems(DNS),

which then matches the domain name with the IP Address and send the IP Details to the Local Computer. Then the Local PC goes to the web-server where files of your desired Website are stored, and then it returns the required data and information of the Website to your browser.

Inside of a DNS Server

XX.YYY.ZZ.EEE   mybusiness.com

172.217.174.238   google.com

Pick a domain name

Picking a Domain Name is one of the most important parts of the Branding. Even if you are starting a business or already have a well-established brand. One most important thing is the Domain Name. According to the statistics, there are more than One Billion Websites currently running over the Internet, so to stand out the crowd, we have to pick a domain name which is catchy, short, and matches to the zing of your business idea.

You may use the following tips to choose the Domain Name for your Business.

- Make it easy to type

- It should be short in length
- Easy to remember
- Avoid Numerals and Special characters in between names
- Do extensive research before
- Act fast to register your domain name as millions are registered every day

Use the appropriate domain name extension. For example, don't use .tech for schools or colleges.

2.2   Finding a domain name

GoDaddy

Allow GoDaddy to assist you in finding the perfect domain name of your choice. Get started with it now, where you will see an enumerable option that will help you choose the best and most appropriate name. Get started with the world's most extensive domain inventory, now managing 80M+ domains with trust and convenience. Search and register the most suitable one for you today and enjoy exciting award-winning with 24/7 phone and chat support. So, get attached, enjoying the best deals at the Lowest Industry Prices. This platform provides the best quality domain names with the minimum cost.

BigRock

Great people have great domain names, and the most valuable domain names are here. Welcome to the most amazing and exciting domain center providing you millions of choices where you will get your domain name as per your need and priorities. Get your.com/.net Domain Name now with two Email Accounts for free. Here it also provides proper DNS management, Domain Registration,24/7 dedicated support to visitors. So, get your perfect match here at low prices. Being aware of cyber crimes here, we also provide Domain Theft Protection, also offer the reliability of working as per suggestions.

Google Domains

Are you searching for the right domain name of your choice? Then check it here. Welcome to the official site of Google Domains and get a custom and reliable domain name of your choice here. Get the domain name and email with google. It provides you a million options; it facilitates 24/7 convenience with phone and chats support, free DNS hosting, and free URL directions. Search and register the name you have been looking for instantly and enjoy exciting offers and the best deals at lower prices. Find your right domain name today.

2.3   Process to register a domain name

A word or phrase can use as a domain name. If you want domain name is for a company, you can put your company name in the domain; it makes it easier to find you on the Internet by your customers.

And always make sure that your domain name is easy to spell out so that the customer can remember your domain name. If domain names are too long, it's difficult to recalled and inclined to user input mistakes.

Try adding a prefix, such as "the" or "my", if your opted domain name is not available.

How to use TLD (Top Level Domain) for a domain name?

In a domain name, on the right of the dot (".") part of the last segment after the final dot is known as Top-Level Domain. The most use Top Level Domains are .com, .org, .edu and .net. There are three types of TLDs:

1. **gTLD (generic top-level domain)**
   - .com – registered by commercial organizations.
   - .net – organizations involved in networking technologies.
   - .org – use for organizations.
   - .gov – only available to bona fide US-based government organizations. US agencies are limited to it.
   - .mil – It's restricted to the military organization of the US government.
   - .edu – intended for educational institutions anywhere in the world.
   - .int – Its use for international organizations and treaty-related purposes.

2. **uTLD (unsponsored top-level domain)**
   - .name – use for individuals and families.

- .info – intended use for informational websites and keep information about a concept, an idea, or your business.
- .biz – use for businesses.
- .travel – restrained for airlines, tourism bureau, and travel agents.

- .mobi – It restrained for sites serving to mobile devices.

3. **ccTLD (country code top-level domain)**
   - .fr – use for France.
   - .ca – use for Canada.
   - .uk – use for the UK.
   - Every country has a top-level domain.

First, decide you are aiming for a local country or planning to go international, then choosing an extension for your domain. If you want to market your business to a precise geographic region, the "country code top-level domain" is a superb choice.

What is Domain Name Registrant, Registrar, and Registry?

The organization or individual registering the domain name is known as Domain Name Registrant. You become the domain name registrant when you submit your request for a domain name.

A registrar is an organization that extracts your registration appeal and keeps your domain for you at the principal registry.

Throughout the registration process, you will be providing information to the registrar. Then the registrar will submit the information to the registry. The registry is also known as the central directory.

The process to register a domain name-
First, you have to choose a domain name to register after you will require to submit a request to a registrar for your domain name registration.

The following information you will require to submit to the registrar:

- Chose a domain name.
- For the domain's registrant, administrative and billing contacts submit information like name and contact information (as well as physical address, email address, and contact phone number).
- Registration term for a domain.
- Information about payment.

Once all this information you have provided to your registrar, the domain name registration process will be initiated. The registrar will send your information of the domain name (including domain name request and the contact and technical information) to the registry.

The contact information for the Whois files by the registry. To the master servers, the registry also includes your domain zone files.

On the Internet, these master servers tell the other servers where your website is stored.

When all the information has updated, your domain is review, registered, and ready to use.

2.4   Getting help with Bluehost

What is Web Hosting?

Whenever it comes to making yourself identifiable, every Organization, Business, School, College needs its website to make themselves available and identified within the globe. In that scenario, Web Hosting comes in play. Web Hosting is just a service that allows you to post your webpage or a set of webpages, also known as a website over the internet. Service providers are also called Web Host or Web Hosting Service Provider.

How does it work?

The Source Code of your website is being stored and hosted on special computers, also known as servers. These servers have an IP address and domain names(you have to buy one), which is a unique name/identification to your website. So if someone types on internet IP or Domain name of your website, the host's computer automatically gets connected to the server where the source code of the website is stored, hence that person can view the website.

Getting started

To host your website, most of the hosting companies need that you have your domain name so that you can host with them. But if you don't have either, you can buy first, or those companies helps you in buying one.

Note: Before buying a Domain name, make sure:

- ⬚ The Domain Name should reflect the idea of the whole business
- ⬚ It should be short, catchy and easy to remember
- ⬚ The domain name extension should match your business, for example, .org for organizations, .com for commercial websites, etc.

Hosting Service Providers various tools like

1. **Personalized Email Accounts**: If you already have your Domain name for your business, for example [www.mybusiness.com], you can create your personal domain email accounts like [your_name@mybusiness.com] with tools provided by your web hosting provider.

2. **WordPress Support:** Wordpress is one of the top Content Management System or CMS, and it is also an online website creation tool. So when you buy a domain, most hosting providers tell you in the very beginning that it's compatible with WordPress or not.

3. **FTP Access:** If you made your website using HTML and upload your code from your local PC to the web server, you would need FTP or File Transfer Protocol. One of the most famous GUI Based FTP Control Panel is Cpanel.

Which plan should I choose?

There are many different Hosting Providers with different Plans. So which plan should you choose? It depends on various factors like

- ⬚ Availability of the Website
- ⬚ Size of the server you have chosen
- ⬚ Scalability of the Resources

⬚ Performance

So if you want to have a high-performance website like an E-Commerce or Food Delivery, you may want to choose Business Hosting. If Speed doesn't matter, like a personal portfolio, you may go with Shared Hosting, in which one web server virtually gets shared with many holders. If you want to use PPU or Pay Per Usage Model, which is ideal for startups, where you don't pay for server size, where you want to pay for the Usage of Resources used, you may go with Cloud Hosting.

Steps to deploy website online:

Step 1: Decide which type of website to build
The essential part of any website is its THEME. First, You have to fix a Theme for a Website, and then you can follow the following steps.

Step 2: Compare Web Hosting Types
There are various ways by which you can choose which kind of

hosting you want to opt for according to performance and cost.

Step 3: Select Hosting Providers and Plans

There are numerous web hosting providers online, like Bluehost, Hostgator, GoDaddy, Dreamhost, hosting, etc. To get started with hosting, we would be taking an example of Bluehost.

a) Create an Account on bluehost.com

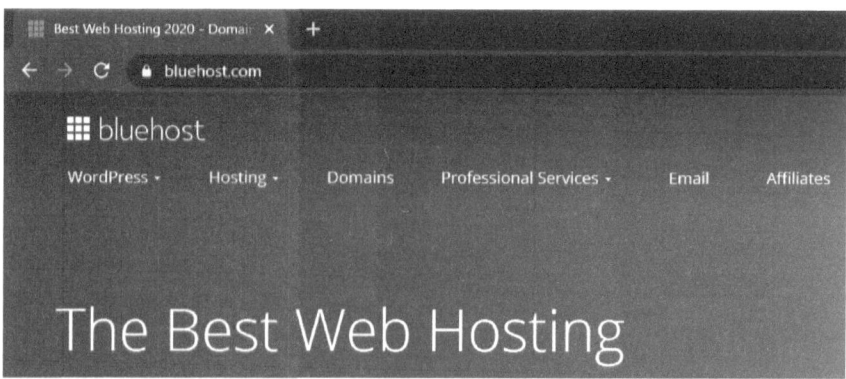

b) Select Your Web Hosting Plan

c) Select and register your domain name

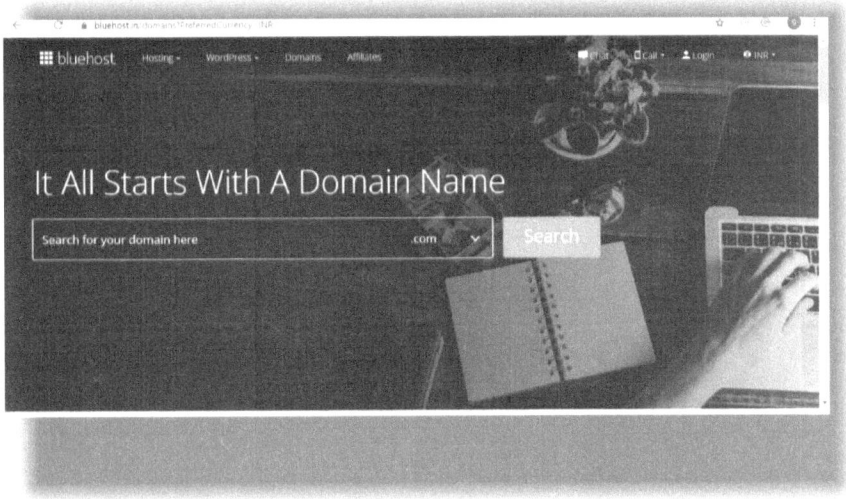

d) After completing your registration process, it hardly takes a few minutes to get instant access. Once you get it, you can start building your website immediately.

e) Start Creating Your Website by Installing WordPress on Bluehost Dashboard

f) The installation form may require some basic information about your site, and the WordPress installation starts. You're good to go.

Install and Configure

3.1   Get started with CPanel

CPanel, which was launched in 1996 by John Nick Koston. It is a web hosting control panel which was developed by American corporation cPanel and L.L.C. The primary purpose of cPanel is to provide services that are required to manage all your web hosting servers. cPanel is a software that gives you the Graphical User Interface (G.U.I.) and different tools that simplify the hosting of your websites.

In this article, we will learn about some basic features of cPanel.

- **Login into CPanel**

To get started with cPanel, you need to log in with a "USERNAME" and "PASSWORD" provided to you by your hosting server.

- **CPanel interface.**

After your successful login, you are landing on the home page, which shows you all the tools and plugins you need to optimize your website or blog. The home page looks similar to the image shown below. However, there may be some differences depending upon the version you are using.

- **Navigation Bar**

Into the navigation bar, there stands a search bar where you can search all your necessary plugins, database, etc., without scrolling down the screen. It will make your job easier.

- **Managing Preferences.**

This section helps you manage, customize your cPanel, and gives you features like updating your contact information and changing your passwords, language, styles, and many more.

- **Web Application**

In this section, cPanel gives you the facility to install different apps. They can be different modules, forums like WordPress, S.M.F., Magento, and much more.

- **Domains**

In this section, you can work with your domain name. Here you can add a new domain, modify the existing domain, or even create a subdomain. To add a new domain name, you need to go in an Addon Domain option where you have to enter your new domain name and some other information.

To modify a domain name, you need to go to the same section, "Addon Domain," select Modify Addon Domain, where you can manage all your domains easily. Also, you can remove your previous domain from here permanently.

- **Emails**

It is one of the best features of cPanel where you can manage and create your customized emails for your websites or blog. You can see various options from the Email section like accounts, spam filter, archive, encryption, autoresponders shown below.

3.2   Installation of Wordpress Using BlueHost

Bluehost is an American company that provides web hosting services for the last 17 years. It serves as one of the largest web hosts which presently hosting. Two million-plus domains.

This article focuses on how we can install WordPress using Bluehost.

- **Open Bluehost.com**

You need to sign in to your Bluehost account. For this, go to Bluehost.com and select "Get Started Now". From here, you redirected to the next page, where you will find different hosting plans. Just choose one according to your convenience.

- **Select a Domain Name**

Now the next step is to select a domain name for your blog or website. However, if you are not sure about the domain name, you can skip this step.

- **Enter your details**

Now at this step, after entering your domain name, you are required to register your details like first and last name, country, phone number, email, country.

- **Review your package**

At this step, you require to check your package and plan information. You can review the add-ons that are added by default and check the extra cost that has attached for services and review which one you need and which one not. The extra charges are for additional securities for your account.

- **Confirm your Payment**

At the last step, you will land on a payment gateway where you need to make payment for your chosen plan. You can pay with your credit card.

- **Install WordPress**

After completion of payment, log in to your Bluehost account and click "My Sites" and then "Create Site". Add your WordPress site name choose domain, and plugins choose a theme and click next. *"Congratulations, you have now installed WordPress using Bluehost."*

Exploring the Wordpress Dashboard

Tour to Wordpress Navigation

There are many online Website Builders and Content management systems over the Internet, but most famous and most preferred from all of them is WordPress. WordPress solution can improve the user's online experience while answering a business's needs for website control, flexibility, and ease of use.

In this section, we will be learning about how we can navigate the WordPress Backend. The back end is your control room. From here, you can share the magic you create with the world. Or put less poetically; from the back end, you can add, edit, and remove the content on your website as well as control what your site looks like.Just login into your WordPress Account as you can already see on this screen there is a lot you can do.

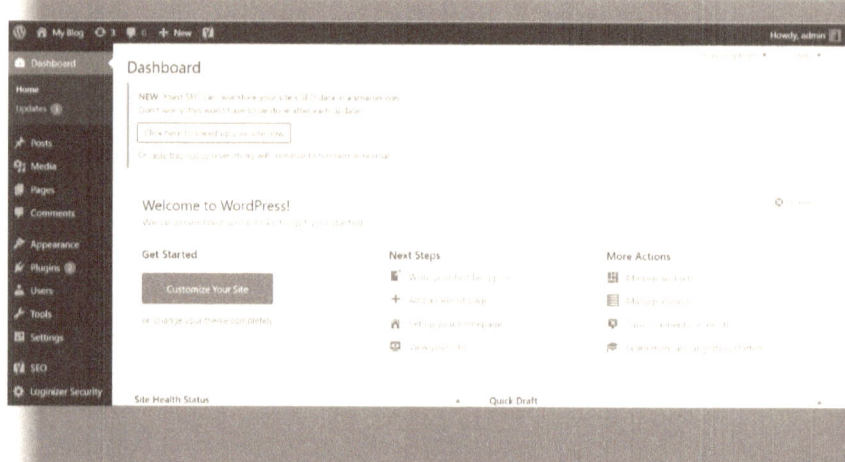

We will go into much more detail on all of the options you see here. At the top of the screen, you can see the toolbar. This toolbar is your administrator toolbar, and it does not appear to people visiting your website.

The first icon you see in the toolbar is the WordPress logo. From here, you can easily access WordPress-related sites and documents. Furthermore, by clicking on the name of your page.

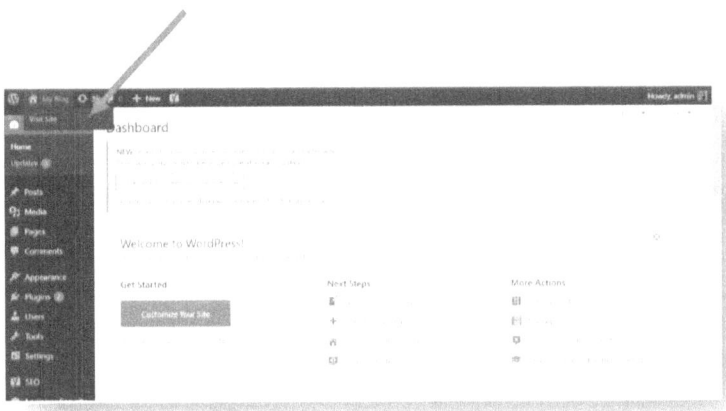

You will be guided to a screen that shows your landing page. This is the thing that your guests see when they go to your site.

You could use this option to see what any changes you've made actually look like. Now let's go back to the toolbar, and see the next option, which allows you quick access to the comments screen.

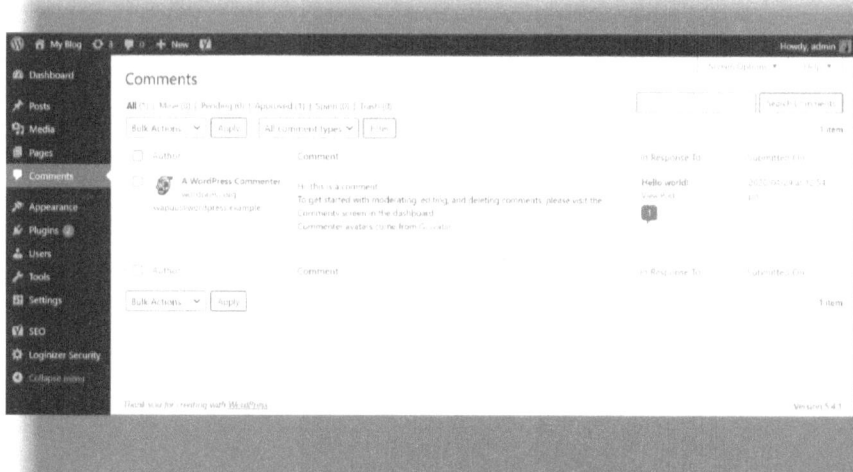

Finally, the toolbar menu Item titled "New" allows you to quickly write new posts, upload new media, write pages, and add new users.

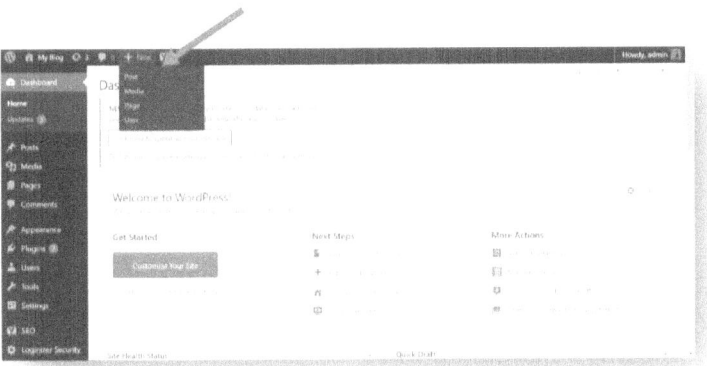

On the right side of the toolbar, you can edit your profile and log out. By clicking your login name or "Edit my profile," you will access the profile screen.

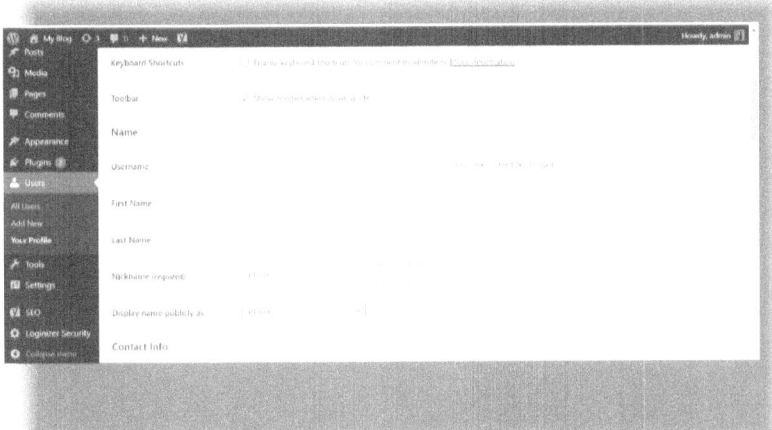

Here you can add some personal information, such as your name and contact info. And most importantly, at the bottom of the screen is where you can change your password. Now that we've seen the toolbar, let's go to the more exciting part: The Dashboard.

When you first logged in with WordPress, you probably saw the welcome message. This message is within a box that we call a dashboard widget. When you are new to WordPress, everything may seem intimidating. So the WordPress developers created this widget with the intention to guide you through the most important first steps you can take in creating your site.

When you first logged in with WordPress, you probably saw the welcome message. This message is within a box that we call a dashboard widget.

When you are new to WordPress, everything may seem intimidating. So the WordPress developers created this widget with the intention to guide you through the most important first steps you can take in creating your site.

Below, you can see that there are a few other widgets as well. Now, the widgets that you see on your dashboard are just the default ones. When you install plugins, other widgets may show up here as well, and that will allow you to manage your site in various ways. But let's quickly see what each of these default widgets provides.

The "At a glance" widget shows you what the current number of your posts, comments, and pages is. It also shows you what version of WordPress you are currently using, as well as the theme that you have activated. You can see that the options for posts, comments, and pages are blue. That means that you can click on them and be taken to their respective editing screens. For a more detailed preview of your posts and comments, there is the activity widget.

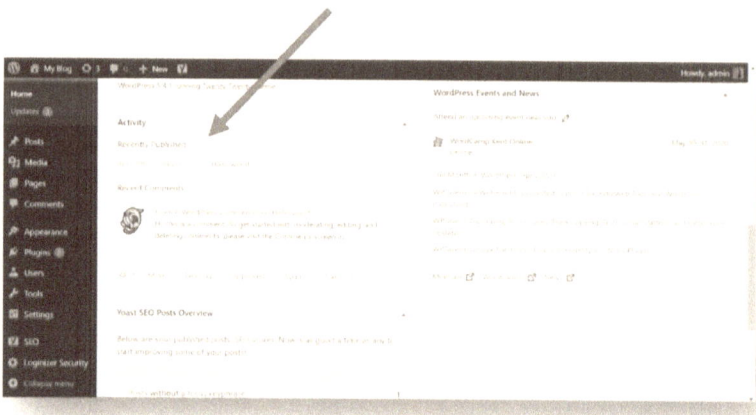

First, you can see the most recent published posts and their titles. Click on them, and you will be taken to the post editing screen, where you can make changes if necessary. Below the recently published posts are the recent comments.

The recent comments section in this widget allows you more than meets the eye. From here, you can see who commented, and access their profile, as well as view the comment, and the post-it relates to. As you may be aware, comments sometimes need managing, and there are plenty of options for that here. For example, you can choose to disapprove, quickly reply, edit, mark as spam, delete or view a comment.

Lastly, this widget gives you an overview and quick access to all the comments on your website.

Moving on to the quick drafts widget. If you have a new post idea, and you want to jot it down quickly, you can do it via the "Quick Draft" widget.

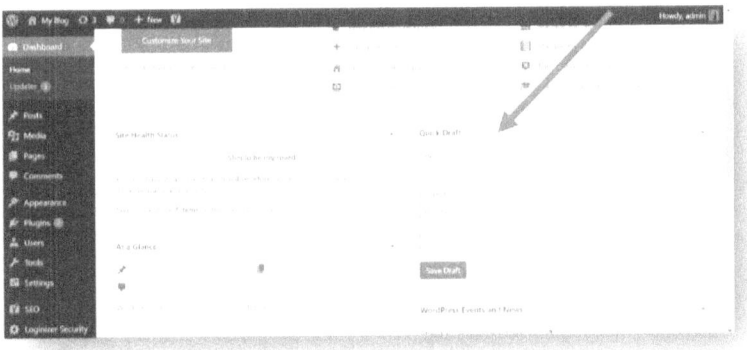

All you need to do is enter a title, write a piece of text, and click save. As the title suggests, this is just a draft, and it will not be published on your site.

Clicking on the link of the draft will take you to the post screen, where you can edit the draft and write a longer, complete version of your idea.

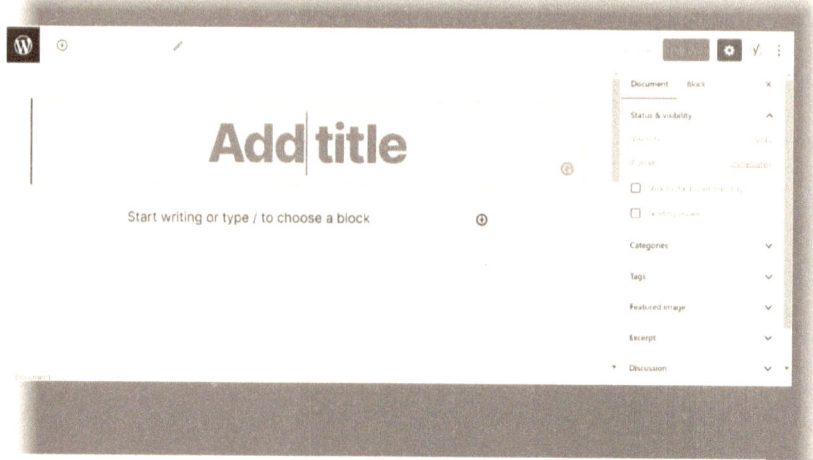

Finally, in the "WordPress News and Events" you are offered a quick glimpse into the WordPress world. By clicking on the links to Meetups, WordCamps, and news.

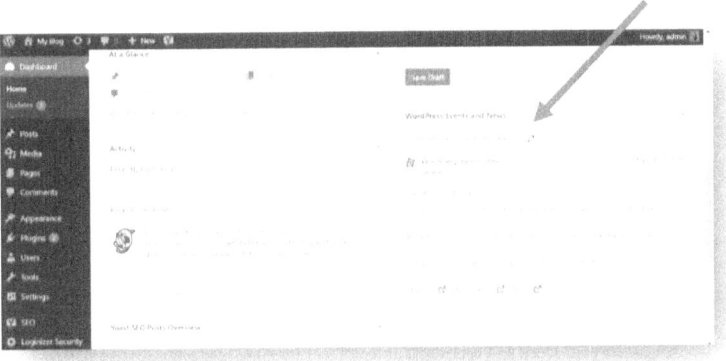

The widgets that we talked about are not static or set in stone. You can easily move, close, open, or delete them from your dashboard. If you hover over the top of one of the widgets, you can see a cross arrow appear.

Every widget has an arrow pointing upwards in the upper right corner. By clicking on the arrow, you will see the widget close or collapse. The arrow is now pointing downwards. If you want to open the widget again, simply click on the downward pointing arrow.

If you want to get rid of a widget completely, you can do that via the Screen Options.

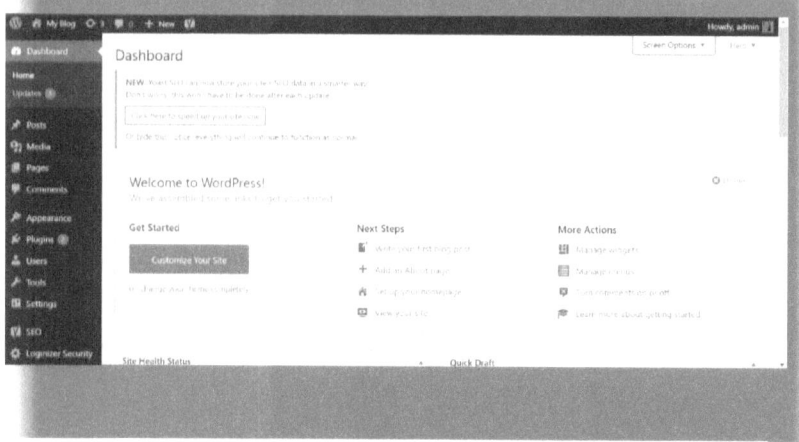

The Screen Options tab is located in the upper right corner below the administrator tab. Click on it, and you will see a menu that contains the widgets we discussed, with ticked boxes next to them. If you untick a box of a respective widget, it will no longer be on your dashboard. If you want to put it back, just tick the box again.

That is your dashboard and all you can do in it.

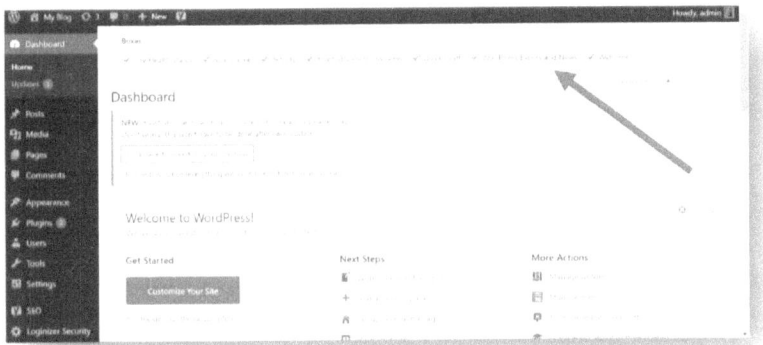

 Note: Always clear the updates from left
Navigation Panel. This will keep the content

4.2   Wordpress tools and settings

WordPress is known for its open-source web hosting services, which makes it easy to design our blogs and websites. As we all are familiar with working on WordPress, we know WordPress brings different tools and settings to customize our blogs and websites. There are various tools and settings available in WordPress, from which some of us are still unaware. Here we are going to discuss some of the essential

WordPress tools and settings that can help build our blogs and website design more accessible and attractive. You can also find tools and settings in your dashboard under respective sections. However, you can also directly search for required settings and tools from the search bar.

WordPress Tools

There are plenty of tools you can get in WordPress. You can see all tools under the Tools section on your dashboard. By default, you see "Available tools" under this section. Just under the Available tools, you can see the two categories: "import" and "export". These two categories of tools we will discuss below.

Import tool contains different scripts used to import data from other CMS (Content Management System) in your WordPress. The export tool contains a script that helps the user to export data into another CMS (Content Management System). The data will export in the form of XML format, which you can import to different WordPress websites or blogs. The exported files contain all your data like your posts, comments, files, categories if any, and tags. Exporting your data to another CMS helps to create a backup for your data.

WordPress Settings

You can find WordPress settings under the "Setting" section on your dashboard. Your settings include maintaining date and time, sites location, who can register. The general settings include:

- **Date Format**

Under this section, you can customize how to display dates on your website or blog, and in what format you want to show them. After choosing your format, you need to save changes to upload the desired format to your website.

- **Time Format**

In this section, you can customize the style of displaying the time on your website. Just select the format and save changes to look for the desired output.

- **Setting up the time zone**

Here you can select the time zone according to your city or country. For example, if you are residing in India, choose New Delhi, and save changes. Now you can see the local time on your website.

- **The week starts in the setting.**

Under this section, you can select the days from the WordPress calendar which you want to start your week. Just select the day from the drop-down menu. By default, Monday will select.

- **Site Language**

By using this setting, we can decide which language your WordPress dashboard will use.

- **A role for the newcomer.**

This section allows you to assign a different role to the new visitor of your website or blog.

- **Memberships**

By selecting this box, you are allowing all the user to create their account on your website or blogs.

- **Site Title**

This setting allows you to enter your site title or name of your blog or website. Different themes use a different format to display the site name.

- **Tagline**

This section allows you to add a punch line to your website's name or your blog name. Remember, always add some catchy taglines to your site to attract traffic.

The following were the few general settings available in your WordPress dashboard. However, there are more different settings available to use about which you can read from various sources on the web.

 Note: You can always fix your per page posts from settings and also check if the search engine by default settings are blocked from WordPress settings. This will create issue on indexing through webmaster.

4.3   Manage users and assign roles

The WordPress roles are nothing but a simple concept used to manage and control what actions (called capabilities) each user of WordPress can perform through the WordPress Dashboard. Webmaster design and organize the roles – which is automatically assigned the administrator when the users were installing WordPress.

The six WordPress Users Permission Roles

There are six default WordPress users permissions roles that you can provide to your users, and those are the following: Administrator, Editor, Author, Contributor, Subscriber, and Super admin. No matter any of the kind of websites you are operating, be it commercial, personal, educational, or of any other kind, user role management is an absolute must require for all types of sites.

1) Administrator: They have full control over the website and have total power with every aspect of the site. They also perform the activities related to adding, editing, and deleting the plugins; with this, they also shape the website looks as well. They also have the control to have access to the site's settings and content management, including posts, pages, and comments.

2) Editor: They have the right to manage the comments, pages, and posts (including those created by the other users). Unfortunately, they have no access to the settings panel, installation of new plugins, nothing in customizing the site's theme, or organizing the other users.

3)Author: Unlike editors, their role is limited to their content management only. Therefore, they have no rights and permissions to approve or delete comments, organize other users' posts, or manage pages. Other than these exceptions, they have the same limited permissions as editors.

4) Contributor: This role of contributor allows the users to add, edit, and delete their content. Other than that, they can't publish, upload media files, and manage their posts after publishing.

5) Subscriber: Their role is only limited to have access to view the published posts or comments and manage their profile section on the Dashboard.

6) Super Admin: The super admin role (only applies to WordPress Multisite network) can perform any administration task within the network, such as adding or deleting the sites, installing a plugin or theme, and organizing content and its settings. They have total control over the network users.

4.4   Takling spam with Akismet plugin installation

- **The purpose of Akismet anti-spam**

Akismet is a very convenient and easy spam filtering service that lets you filter the spam from all the comments, submissions, trackbacks, forms, and contact form messages that unwantedly drop down into your sites. The filters work as by combining all the information related to spam, which gets captured on all the participating sites, and then the spam rules are used to block all the spam presently and also to block all the spam that will appear in future. The Akismet is the feature that is offered by the Automattic, the company behind Wordpress.com.

- **How to get Akismet anti-spam**

You need first to install and activate the Akismet Anti-spam Plugin; these are the two easy steps to use the Akismet anti-spam plugin:

1) You need to access your WordPress dashboard, and then following it. It would be best if you went to the Plugins menu. Then you have to go to select add new and type 'Akismet Anti-Spam' on the search bar

2) Then all you have to do is click on Install Now, and then just hit Activate.

- **The Akismet action to check spam**

Akismet is what that provides WordPress with the ability to work on the comments and submissions against their global database of spam. A WS form PRO is fully integrated with the popular Akismet spam check plugin, which provides its users a convenient, reliable, and effective way of tackling the fraud comments and all the form submissions that contain the spam content which adversely affects your content.It works like this that any of the comments or submissions that include the 'Spam Check with Akismet' action will get highlighted and graded form spam, and also, a colored circle will accompany the fraud content and unmeaningful submissions in the WS Form submissions page.

- **Activation of Akismet Plugin**

To fight against spam through Akismet, you will need to have your Akismet Plugin to be activated and to be for an Akismet API Key. These API keys are surely free for personal blogs for everyone, but for all kinds of businesses and other commercial sites, it needs the paid subscriptions. If you have not registered for API Keys or if not installed the Akismet Plugin, the Akismet action for spam-check will not be available to you to choose when configuring actions for your form.

- **Need to Stop spam**

The WordPress comment spam and the registration spam has always been a massive problem for all the present WordPress users. Just not this also that for some of the WordPress websites, it is pervasive to receive hundreds or even thousands of spamscomment every week very much recently. This level of spam, which they encounter recently, can surely the reputation with and the commentators if we are failing to tackle it. Therefore, it has become essential to face the spam and overcome it head to head and thwart all their attempts of spamming your website.

- **Some Pro tips to stop spam**

The pro tips to overcome spam are as follows:

1) Configuring Discussion Settings: It is that before you install any anti-spam plugin to overcome spam, you should configure WordPress discussion settings properly.

2)Disable Member Registration: Then, it is understandable that you should disable the member registration in the general settings, which will reduce the registration spam.

3) Then finally, at last, it comes to the ultimate solutions that are anti-spam plugins, which you can use to tackle spam thoroughly. There are different anti-spam plugins such as

Akismet, WP-Spam Shield anti-spam, Antispam Bee, etc....
which you can use to overcome spam.

4.5   Setting up coming soon page by seed prod plugin

Plugins are software components that are used to add or extend the functionality of our software products, blogs, or websites. There are various plugins available for different use. WordPress, which is known for its open-source services for web hosting, uses various plugins to enhance the functioning of our website or blog. We all are familiar with the different plugins we use to create our WordPress website and blogs. One of the famous and most widely used plugins is "seedprod". We will discuss this plugin in this article.

Have you ever imagined that you can increase traffic to your blog or website even before launching it? Since traffic is an essential part that plays a vital role in increasing the popularity of your website. Seedprod uses for the same task. Using this plugin, you can create a coming soon page, which helps you to create a promotion for your website, which is under process. You can use different themes and color combinations to create some awesome coming soon page.

Steps to create a coming soon page:

- **Choose the plugin**

To start building a coming soon page, you need to choose a proper plugin. We will be using Seedprod to create our coming soon page. The icon of the plugin looks similar to the image shown below.

- **Install and Activate the Plugin.**

Click on the install button below and after installing activate the plugin.

- **Create a new coming soon page.**

After installing and activating the plugin, open the seedprod plugin, and select status to enable coming soon mode. After that, select "edit coming soon maintenance page".

You can choose themes from all available themes. Don't worry; you will have plenty of options to choose according to your website. You can also select an empty template to start designing your theme for your coming soon page.

- **Adding your content to the page**

After selecting the theme, start adding content to your page from various options. Using Seedprod page editor, you can easily add content to your page.

- **Customize your background**

Here you can customize your background image. Here you can choose the image you want to display when someone sees your coming soon page. Also, you can change your image setting by clicking "Background Advance Setting".

- **Editing your page**

Here you can edit the page colors, font style, and modify your buttons, if any.

- **Creating a contact form**

You can also create a contact form to create the audience. You need to go to contact form setting and select Enable Contact Form.

- **Adding a countdown timer**

This is another exciting feature to attract your audience by adding a countdown timer so that people visiting your blog or website can know when your website or blog will be launching. Just select enable countdown and select your time zone and format you need to display.

- **Social Share**

This is another way to enhance the promotion of your website. By enabling the social share button, you get features to share your coming soon page to various social platforms. You get options like Twitter, Facebook, LinkedIn.

- **The Progress Bar**

This section shows that in what time your website or blog will be launching.

These were some basic features that you can add to your coming soon page using Seedprod plugin. There are many other features too that you may add according to your requirements.

Creating Wordpress Website

Wordpress theme from scratch

Here we are discussing how one can create a WordPress theme from Scratch. So, know you are familiar with the topic, so let's understand what a theme is? A theme is a collection of different templates that are combinations of different colors, styles, etc., that define your website's appearance. WordPress has various themes, and you can choose one that describes your website the best. Here we will be discussing all information related to WordPress themes.

When you install the WordPress on your system from WordPress.org, you get some pre-installed themes. You can check them under appearance, followed by themes. You need to install the theme of your choice that you wish to add to your blog or website. Not sure how to do so. There is a simple way; search for your website's type in the search bar, and WordPress will show all relevant themes related to your website or blog, and you may choose the one that best fits your website. Now WordPress facilitates you to customize the pre-defined themes according to your choice. To do this follow these steps:

- Go to Appearance.
- Select the themes option.
- Select the theme you want to customize.
- After selecting the theme, click on the customize button.

After clicking on the customize button, you will see a new page opens, and you will find many different options on the left side of the page. Here you can define colors, the identity of your site, taglines for your website, menus, widgets, etc. Now, this was all about the default themes that are provided by WordPress. However, WordPress allows you to design and create your theme and upload it to your website or blog. Now let's discuss how we can do that.

Creating a WordPress Theme from Scratch

To create a WordPress theme from scratch, you need to create a new folder and name it with the name you want to create your theme. There must be a style.css file to create your theme. Now, at the starting of the file, you can add comments so that you know what your file defines.

To add a comment using "/*" and to end the comments use "*/". Now you need to add two more files that are functions.php and index.php. Finally, you can now activate your theme. To activate the theme, you must have WordPress Installation.

Now you are ready to upload your theme to your WordPress website for this login to your WordPress account with your Username and Password. After login to your account, go to the Appearance section and select the theme, and you will find your theme in the theme section. You can also search for the theme by the name you have given when creating the file. But you will not find any images in your theme as we haven't added any image yet to our theme. To add an image to your theme, upload the image in the media section, and from there, you can access the images and add them to your theme.

You can also add a background image to your theme. For this:

- Go to the Appearance section and select the theme.
- After that, select the customize option.
- A new page opens, which displays many options to customize your theme on the left side.
- Scroll down, and you will see the background image option select that.
- A new window opens, and you can see a section to select an image click that button, and you will then be landing at WordPress media library where you can choose the image.
- At last, click on the choose image button, and as soon as you do that, the window closes, and you can see the image you selected in your background.

You can add customized background images by using the "Full-Screen Background pro" plugin. If you are good at coding, you can use CSS to add custom background images to your theme in WordPress. You can refer to various CSS tutorials and WordPress tutorials to learn how you could add a customized background in your blog or website using CSS.

To customize images to your theme, follow the following steps:

- **Working on function.php file**

To add an image to your theme, you need to add a shortcode to your function.php file on your website or blog. You can find the function.php file in the appearance section followed by the editor and then edit the function.php file. You just need to add "add_theme_support('post-thumbnail size', width, height);". You need to specify the width and height of the images you want to enter.

- **Displaying custom size**

In this step, you need to display the sizes you want in your theme. To do this, go to the theme file, and there you will find a post loop. Add the below code line in that post loop:

<?php the_post_thumbnail('your-specified-image-size'); ?>

In the above code, you must write the size of the image you wish to have in your theme.

- **Finalizing your task**

After you have added code for the required files, you need to reorganize the thumbnails. Doing this will change the size of the images that have uploaded previously.

It was all about creating a theme from scratch in WordPress. However, there are many more ways to do the same task. It depends on individuals' choice of which one to go for.

5.2   Customizing your free themes and layouts

Working on WordPress is an easy task. However, it becomes more comfortable when you get more than 200 themes for free. WordPress provides you with a large variety of items you can use for websites or blogs. You have many options to choose from for your website. Still, you are not happy with the theme you select, the Appearance of the item. Well, in that case, you need not worry because WordPress has the solution to this problem also. WordPress allows you to customize your themes as per your requirements. You can also customize the layout of your home page in WordPress. Here we will discuss how we can tailor our item and designs in WordPress.

To customize your theme, follow the steps discussed below:

- **Select your theme**

First of all, you need to select the theme you want to add to your website or blog. For this, go to Appearance and select items. You will be landed on a themes page where you can see many themes. Choose one from those or search one from the search bar and click activate.

- **Customize the theme**

Now it's time to customize your WordPress theme. To start customizing, go to Appearance and select customize. You can see the list of available options on the left side of your screen when you open the personalized page. The right side will also give you a preview of the customization you are adding to your website.

- **You are modifying your site tagline and title**

A tagline is a punch line used to attract visitors. To add or modify the tagline, go-to site identity and add the text you want to display at your website. After finishing, click on the save and publish button.

- **Other customization**

You can also add different customization to your site, depending upon the theme you are using. The various customization available is changing the header image, color combinations, menus, buttons, and many more from the list. After completion of customization, first preview the theme on the right side, and if the results are satisfactory, click on save and publish button to save the changes and upload the customized theme to your website.

A home page is the first page that pop-ups when the visitor opens your website or blog. The home page must be attractive and easy to understand for the user. WordPress also allows you to customize the home page. You can follow these steps to customize the home page of your site:

- **Add a Home Page**

You first need to add a home page to your website or blog. To do this, go to the dashboard and select pages. Now click the "Add New" button and name the page as the home page.

- **I am customizing the home page**

There are two ways to customize the home page for your website.

1. We are changing the layout using a theme.

Go to dashboard select appearance and then click on widgets. Here you can see many options like- footer, header, sidebars. You can select the options and start customizing them.

2. Using the Page Builder Plugin

Plugins make your task easy in customization of your home page. Just install the plugin and activate it. You can use any of the plugins from different plugins available on WordPress like Beaver, Divi, element. These plugins consist of thousands of home page templates that you can use. You need to install the guide, and to customize them, you have different select and implement tools that you can use to customize and replace the content of the home page with a single click.

5.3 Managing categories and subcategories for starting a blog

Many people around the globe want to start blogging, or in simple words, they want to share their stories, learnings, etc. to the world. When they complete their first blog, their post doesn't have that professional touch of a blog. It happens because of their blog lack structure. If you are one of them, then this article we will explain to you how to organize your blog posts to make it more expressible, enjoyable to read and more engaging.

- **How to organize Your Blog in WordPress:**

Organizing your blog post help the reader to find relatable content more efficiently and make your content more engaging. A properly categorized blog help reader to get a complete picture of what they will get if they spent their precious time to read it. Here categories refer to general topics in a post.

In WordPress, categories can be listed on navbar or somewhere on the homepage as a link depending on the theme you choose to publish the blog. When a reader clicks on one of the link they will be redirected to a page where they get lists of all the post related to that category. Here you also have the option to not assign any category to your post. If you don't assign any category to some of your posts, then those post will get a category of "uncategorized" if you don't assign a category to any post then you won't get any category on navbar or somewhere else.

How to categorize your post:

Follow the steps to categorize your new or previous post: -

- When you add a new post, you will an option of "categories & Tags" in the right sidebar of "Post Setting", there you will have all the option to "uncategorized", "Add New Category" to your post.
- To change categories of your previous posts, follow the steps: -
- Go to sites > posts, and then click on the post to go to the editing page of that of the particular post.
- When you are in editing page you will have an option as explained above.

When you are in editing page, to add post to your blog in subcategory, you need to click on "Add New Category" and then disable "Top-level Category" and then choose a parent category. Now you can write your subcategory name and then press enter or click on "Add".

With the option explained in 1., you will also be able to uncategorized your post by just checking the square box before "uncategorized".

After changing or adding the category, you need to click "Publish" or "Update" to reflect the changes in the respective post. If you have added a new category in your blog and added some post under that category, then a new category link will be added automatically to your WordPress website.

5.4   Publishing your first post

It will help you to start your individual and executive educator blog. The primary purpose of this step is to help you to acknowledge how personal blogs used posts. Give tips to you on how to write useful posts, and you can learn how to publish your first posts.

What are Posts?

Your main content will be publishing on your posts, such as your ideas and information, which you want to share with others. The most recent post always shows at the top of the page. In a post you include:

- **Title of the post** – This will make it easier for the reader to know about the post and acknowledge the reader's attention to read your post.
- **Post publishing date** – At the top of the post, you will see the publishing date of a post.
- **The post was written by** – Post author name will display in the post. If you have not changed your display name, your username will be automatically displayed.
- **Content of the post** – This is the content part of the post where you provide the primary information that you want to share with others. It can also include texts, images, videos, and links, etc.

- **Comments** – This would contain the response part where readers can write their views about your post and share their thoughts.

Who Publishes the posts ?

On other blogs, the posts are published by just one educator, while on the educator blogs, you will see some are group blogs where specific individuals publish posts on the blog.

Personal educator blogs are more common because, due to individual ownership, most of the people are more interested in posting on their blog.

Examples of group blogs are The Edublogger, Connected Principals, and Two Writing Teachers.

Give Instructions about how to publish a new post?

You can publish a post by the following steps:

1. First, go to posts.

2. Then click "Add New" to add a new post.

3. Then give a title to your post.

4. And then add your content in the post which you want to share with others.

5. Add your tags and categories.

6. When you finished your writing, click "Publish".

7. Now, your post will display on your blog so that others can read.

What is the use of Previewing your Draft?

It is a good idea to use a preview option before you publish your post so you can see what it looks like to your readers. By clicking on "Save Draft", you preview a post and then click "Preview". Then a new tab of your post opens up in a draft version. If you want to make any changes, go back to your draft and change it.

5.5   Difference between post and pages

Creating a website is only the first task that you have completed. The main thing that runs your website is traffic. Now, the question arises what makes people visit your website? Well, the answer is simple. It's the content that you upload to your site. Yeah, your website's content is an essential thing that you need to keep in mind that your content should be relevant. It is the content that brings traffic to your website. Now how do you create content? Well, there are two ways to create content for your website that is posts and pages. Now you might be wondering both of them do the same thing, then what is the difference between the two? So let's discuss the difference between posts and pages.

Posts

The post is the content that you publish in the form of articles, documents, images, etc. Have you ever gone through your social media account like Instagram or Facebook? You keep adding photos and videos to your account and share them with friends. That is an example of a post. The post you publish on your website has a date, and it has been arranging in reverse. That is, the last post you have posted is displayed first, and the first one goes last in the list. The position on your website can be differentiated into different categories. For example, if you are posting something related to the food, you can categorize it into veg and non-veg. You can also add tags to your post that helps the reader to find the most relevant content that they are looking for them. The article typically comprises a title, the date it has published, and the writer's name, comments, categories, and tags. Jobs are updated frequently.

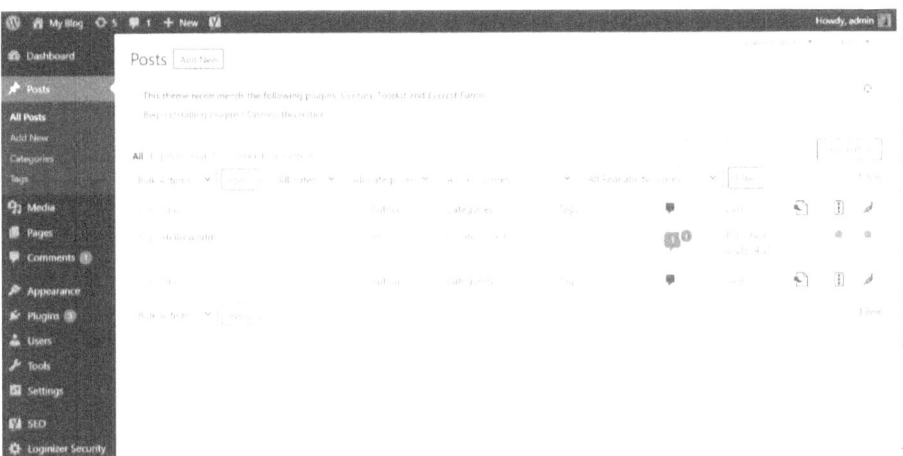

Pages

Pages, on the other hand, are slightly different from the post. You don't need to update your pages frequently. Pages usually contain static content. You can have too many posts on your website, but adding too many pages to your site can make users find their content difficult. Most frequently added pages are terms and condition page, about us page, contact us page. The pages cant categorized as in the post; instead, you can relate one page to another. The page does not contain Publish

date, author name, etc.

Shortcuts to Wordpress Website

6.1 Schedule posts for long run

Posts are essential content of your websites. The type of post can vary depending upon the type of site you have. Post can be in the form of articles if you own a website that provides information to different topics, images if you own a website that shows a collection of various items or the combination of images and content. The post on your website published in reverse order, with the most recent one at the top and the old ones at last. We will be discussing how one can schedule his or her posts to update the website regularly.

If you are creating a website, you cannot randomly write and post anything on your website. To generate traffic and increase your website's popularity, you need to keep regularity in posting your content. Whenever you post something on your website, you or your visitors can see that post, but google keeps track of everything you do on your website. Even if you do not update anything on your website, google notices that also, and when google notices that for a long time, there have been no updates on your website, it considers that your website is no more and google stops showing it to others. But maintaining the regularity in your posts doesn't seem an easy task as it looks. So to ease this, WordPress comes with a facility to schedule your posts. When you schedule the posts, you need not log in to every time to post something. Instead, it is done by WordPress at regular intervals of time. Now the question comes that how can you schedule your posts on WordPress. There are three ways in which you can schedule your posts, and we will discuss them one by one.

1. **Scheduling by using a plugin**

Using a plugin makes a task easy. Two different plugins can use to do the job.

- **CoSchedule**

Using this plugin helps you to manage all your blog posts, marketing, social media content. You need to download the plugin and need to pay for the different plans you wish to use.

- **WP Scheduled Posts**

This plugin helps you to access more advanced scheduling features. WP Schedule adds a calendar to your dashboard fast and easy scheduling.

2. Using a Block Editor

It is the simplest way to schedule the post. Open the post you want to schedule and on the right sidebar go to documents. There you will find "status and visibility" it is set to immediate. Click that, and it will open a calendar, and from there, you can set the date and time for posting your post.

3. Using a Classic Editor

If you are using the older version of WordPress editor, you can still schedule your posts. Just go to the post you wish to schedule and select the publish widget. By default, it will get set to "immediately." Click edit and set the date and time you wish to upload your post. After that, select the schedule button and done.

Note: You can use "advanced scheduled post" plugin or "Wp Schedules posts". These are preferred by bloggers for maintain posts.

6.2   Page Design by Elemenator

When we want to start blogging, create an online community for our YouTube channel, etc., we need to build a separate website that will tell us and help us build a strongly connected community. Now, comes a list of questions, how are we going to build that professional webpage, we don't know how to code, we don't know how to host, etc. Don't worry; we are going to explain to you how to do all of that even if you have no idea about coding, hosting, etc.

Elementor is WordPress's visual page builder plugin to build a professional web page on WordPress live using just drag and drop. It's straightforward to use because of the visual method of the creation of web pages.

What is Elementor:

Elementor is a WordPress page builder. It works by integrating with your WordPress account. It comes with a bundle of amazing themes that can use to create any types of dynamic webpages we can imagine; it can create an amazing custom landing page, sales pages, promotional pages, and even custom forms. With elementor, you will be able to develop responsive pixel perfect design, animate your elements, etc. you also have options to make your page dynamic like a custom search bar, contact form, etc.

The main benefits of using these WordPress plugins are:

- Earlier in WordPress, when we want to change something we have to go to settings of the theme, edit it as we desire, publish it and then we have to refresh the page to see the changes, but with Elementor we will be able to see all the changes visually and live.
- Almost all of the WordPress themes have different options in setting to edit the look of a page as we desire, but no themes had all of the options. There you require to code to get the desired output on the page, but with a page builder like Elementor, we can go to live to edit of the page where we will be able to drag and drop the section or element where we want and edit live all the images and text.

- We can also build a WordPress page from scratch without any pre-built themes; you need to drag and drop the elements on the blank canvas and change the sidebar settings to get the desired look.

How to Get Started:

As we have a brief idea about what is elementor and what it is capable of, now we will dive in deep to know how to use it to create an amazing web page. In this section, we will learn step by step to get started with the elementor.

Like all other WordPress plugins, we need to install it in our wordpress. There are two ways to install it:

1. By downloading elementor through its official website:
- Go to the official webpage of elementor, enter details to log in, and download it.
- Go to WordPress dashboard plugins > install plugins.
- Upload the downloaded zip folder
2. By WordPress dashboard: -
- Go to WordPress dashboard plugins or if the theme supports this plugin.

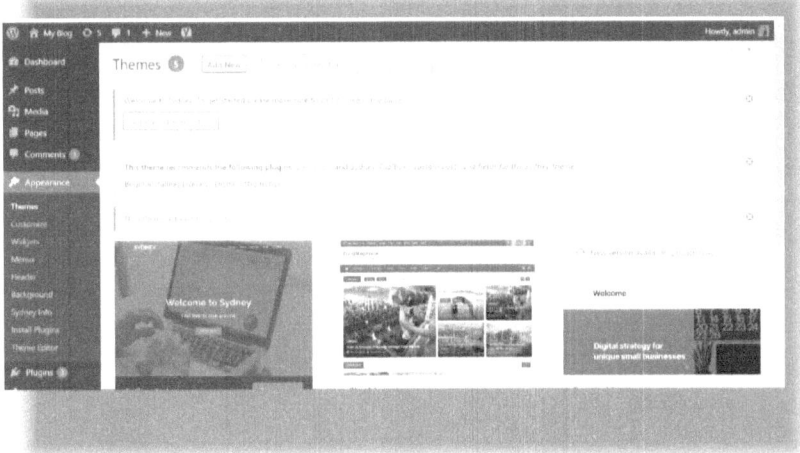

- Enter elementor in the search field.
- Install elementor and after installation activates it.

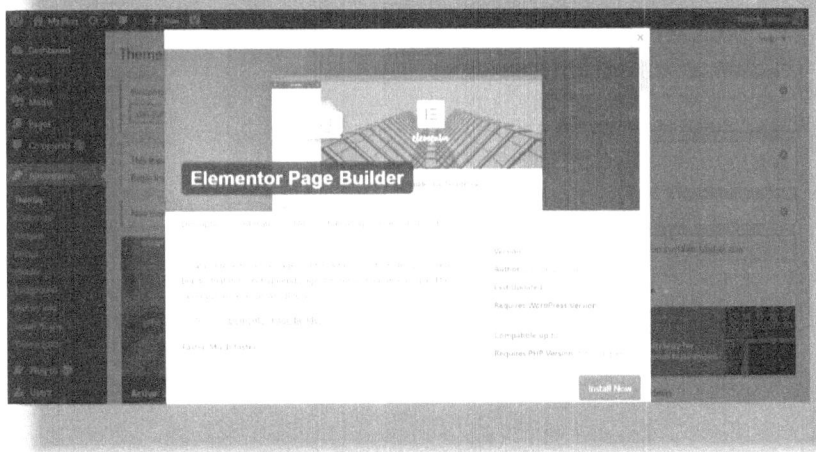

After the installation is complete, we are good to go and edit and create any webpages we want.

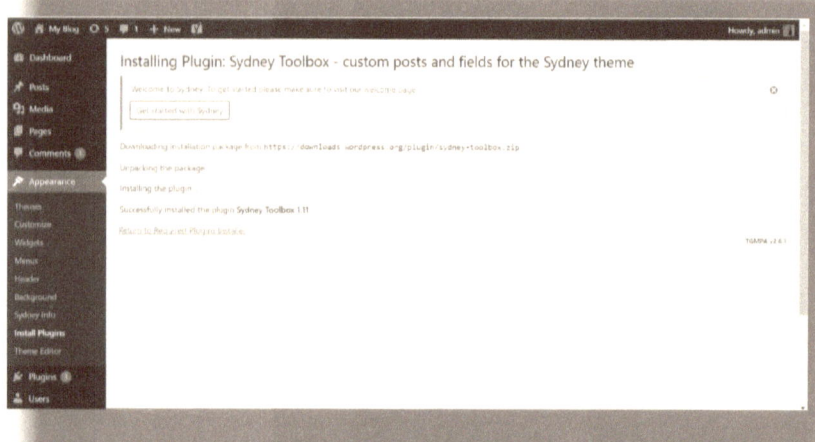

We can access the elementor editing page by either going to plugin > elementor or by clicking on "add with elementor" when we create or edit posts on wordpress.

On the editing page of the elementor, we have to drag and drop features on the left side of the editor. We can also search for specific widgets that we would like to add to our pages.

If we want to edit a pre-built theme, we have two buttons to add to any theme we like to edit.

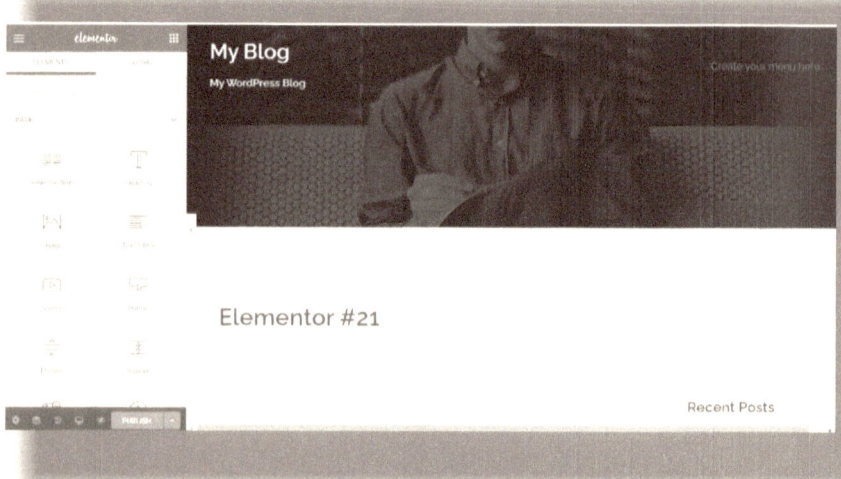

The first button is of "+" sign that will give access to 300+ designers-made elementor themes, and the second is a "folder" logo that will allow you to open a theme from your local computer that you have decided to edit.

Now we have opened a theme to edit; we can hover over elements and click it to open settings of that particular element or text or images on the left sidebar of the editing page. If we want to add a new element or section, we have particular widgets to drag it in place, and that particular section will get added. The setting will also be available in the left sidebar to edit that section.

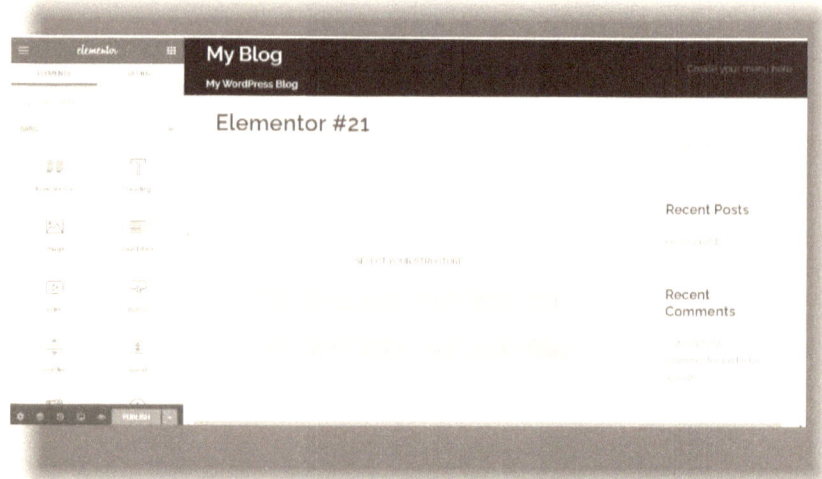

There is also an option to create a new webpage from scratch; to do that, we need to open a new canvas and drag and drop section or element on the canvas and edit accordingly to create a stunningly beautiful dynamic webpage.

Upload media and content on the sections dragged and dropped on the screen.

Update text and create a website landing page as per the requirement of the business.

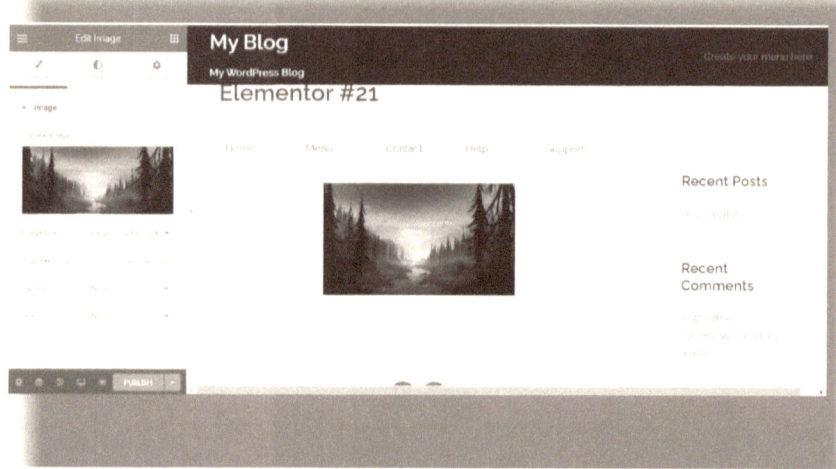

You can also use some predefined libraries for the template of the few sections,

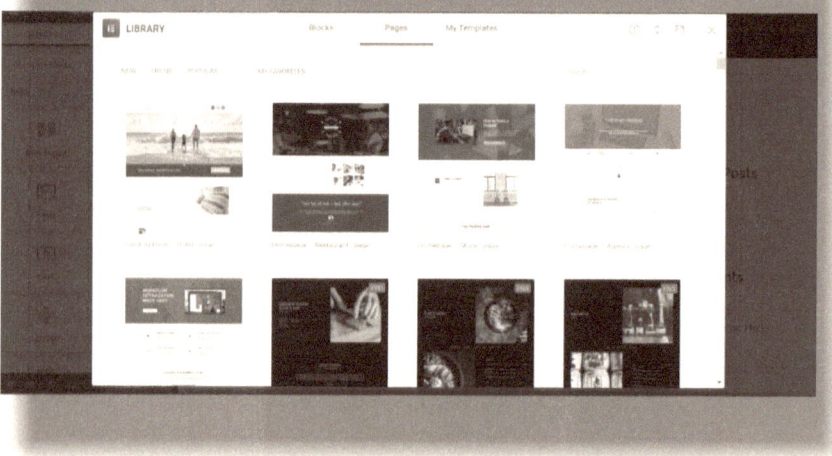

Features of Elementor:

Elementor comes packed with lots of features that are easy to use and will give you the ability to put down your imagination on a web page. With elementor, you will have all the options that you want in a dynamic webpage.

Let's discuss the important feature of elementor that we will need to create a professional dynamic web page.

- It has 300+ professionally designed templates and 90+ widgets to create content you need, like buttons, headlines, forms, images, etc.

- It has a popup builder to create popup according to your imagination, like opening an image slider. At the same time, click on one of the images in the gallery you created or any warning like wrong input fields.

- A responsive editor will allow us to open your page in the mobile view, and we can tweak the element as we want.

- We can also create an online store with WooCommerceBuilder (one of the features of elementor)

- We can make our background alive, adding amazing videos to the background of our section.

- Almost all of the basic CSS properties are available in elementor to edit our element like a pro. E.g., box-shadow, CSS filter, positions, blend modes, etc.

- We can also add SVG icons smart, flexible, and light icons in any size.
- We can also add custom CSS that can be applied globally to all our pages.
- With form widgets, we can create all types of live forms without worrying about backends and coding.
- We also have to lots of options for layouts while we are creating a page from scratch. Features like column width, column gap, z-index, content position, margin, padding, etc. will help you to customize layouts of your webpage.
- To add the professional web page content, we have the following options: nav menu widget, login form widget, search widget, posts widget, WordPress comment

 Note: Elementor can have some pre loader but you can remove this earlier to avoid blank space which is sometimes experienced on the

6.3   Essential Pages (Privacy Policy, Terms and Conditions)

Essential pages are a necessary part of your website. It is mandatory to include crucial pages on your website or blog irrespective of the type of site you have, whether it is a big e-commerce website or a small scale blog. Essential pages define the norms and conditions that the user of the website should strictly follow. Let's discuss some of the necessary pages you need to have on your site:

1. Privacy policy

It is the most important page that you should include on your website. Some countries have made it a strict rule that one should add a privacy policy page on his or her website. The main aim of the privacy policy page is to inform the website visitors and users of how the website deals with the information they have provided to them. However, if you don't include a privacy policy page on your website or blog, you may be caught for not following the rule and can be sent to court as well in the worst case.

There are various platforms where you can create a privacy policy page for your website:

- Free Privacy Policy
- PricavyPolicy.com
- Shopify
- IUBENDA
- Trust Guard

You can refer to any of those websites to generate the best privacy policy page for your website.

1. **Terms and Conditions pages**

It is mandatory to inform your users that they need to follow specific rules that you have defined to use your website. Here comes in the role this page that describes the terms and conditions when a new user joins your website. Directly terms and condition page is an agreement that each user of the site or blog has to agree with before using the Website. You can create your own customize terms and conditions, or you can refer some online platform to do so for your website like getterms.io and so on.

2. **Contact Us page**

This page describes the website or blog. Contact Us page contains the information that the user of the website can refer to contact the officials of the website. Usually, the Contact Us page includes companies email address, contact number, and address where the user can reach if he or she faces any problem while using the website. The blog's owner can add a short description of himself if it is a personal blog.

3. **About Us page**

This page defines the website, its functional areas, the central authorities who run the website. The page also explains the goals of the organization.

 Note: Bloggers with hands on experience suggests having privacy policy, about us,

6.4   OptimizePress for funnel lead generation

OptimizePress is a product that comes as a WordPress module that is utilizing to manufacture sites pointed towards lead age and conversion of sales.

OptimizePress

Home   Product   Templates   Blog   Support   Log In   Demo

The WordPress Page Builder Made for Marketers, Coaches & Creators

Create landing pages, sales pages, and funnels with our complete
marketing suite for WordPress

Get Started Now >   Watch a Demo ▶

It is easy to use the software that has been helping
entrepreneurs throughout the years make select in pages,
points of arrival, sales pages, and enrollment entries.

Many greeting pages configure formats and components for
all clients of OptimizePress, which permits them to come out
with a sweet glancing plan in a matter of moments.

OptimizePress accompanies several highlights that are
anything but difficult to execute into your site or point of
arrival. One reason why OptimizePress happened to be a

pleasant decision for most online advertisers is that it's anything but difficult to learn and execute.

Highlights of OptimizePress

Streamline has barely any highlights that may be of incredible enthusiasm to you. See them underneath:

- **Boundless pages**

OptimizePress empowers you to make parts and heaps of pages (points of arrival, sales pages, and so on.) unbounded, on each site you've offered a permit to.

There are additionally in-built templates which makes it simple for you to complete your pages quicker, and they are partition into classes:

- Landing Pages
- Deals pages
- Online course pages
- Opt-in pages.
- Much thanks to you pages
- Enrollment site pages

All of these page layouts centered around a particular objective for your business; however, you can alter them any way you need.

- **Facilitated on WordPress**

OptimizePress works just with WordPress sites, which warrants you to have your self-facilitated site.

You can introduce OptimizePress as a WordPress topic or add it as a module. You'll approach everything required when you present it.

- **Extraordinary components**

With the OptimizePress LiveEditor, where the fundamental altering and planning happens, you can include significant components such as catches, sound players, video players, commencement clocks, boxes, tributes, and others. There are more noteworthy components in the Distributer and Ace arrangement holders where they gain admittance to the PlusPack elements, making it conceivable to add item grandstands and sliders to your pages.

- **A/B split testing**

Utilizing the OptimizePress Experimental module, you can think about at least two varieties of your page plans.

At that point, you can conclude which will probably bring more amount.

- **Participation site**

This product includes a participation site highlight called Upgrade Part module. Answerable for securing your substance and permits you to offer access to individuals.

Pros of OptimizePress

- **One time charge option**

It is a beneficial side! You don't have to make a fuss over a month to month charges for utilizing this instrument. Pay once, and you can use it forever.

- **Ideal for content makers**

OptimizePress is the best and most recommendable sales funnel manufacturer and greeting page programming for Bloggers, Publicists, or other substance makers. On account of its engaging alternatives, WordPress is facilitating, and Web optimization agreeableness.

• Simple to be learned by anybody

OptimizePress likewise utilizes intuitive supervisors like the most point of arrival software. This component makes it simple to learn.

• Less Expensive

Since you don't have to continue paying on a month to month premise, OptimizePress perhaps the least expensive sale funnels and greeting page developers out there.

• You have control

With OptimizePress, you'll have more command over your site and pages, which is Dissimilar to ClickFunnels, where all your business is facilitating on their database. As per who is hosting this, 27% of the all-out locales on the web have controlled by WordPress, and it makes up 14% of the best 100 sites on the planet.

That implies you're probably going to be in safe hands while on WP.

Building funnel for lead generation

A marketing funnel is usually a start, middle, and end of the customer journey. These stages would sometimes refer to as the top, middle, and bottom of the funnel. How the consumer sees in this process depends on the deals you make and the sort of marketing funnel that you use.

Top: This is usually a landing page wherein returns for some types of the lead multiplier or free trial, we request for name and email.

Middle: This is when you foster the relationship and build a relationship with your new subscriber. Creating a bond of trust and trust with your new subscriber will give them a greater right to turn to a paying customer when you market your goods.

Bottom: You usually make a selling bid to your subscribers at this point in the funnel. The generosity and value you've provided in the funnel's previous stages will significantly increase the chances to convert a subscriber to a customer successfully.

OptimizeFunnels

Using the selection of pre-created funnels takes just a few mouse clicks to have a completely built, linked and configured funnel.

One great feature of OptimizeFunnels is that the new OptimizePress 3 lightning page builder works seamlessly. It means a limited learning curve is in place, so you can quickly create your funnels.

The WordPress funnel builder OptimizeFunnel has developed so that you can also customize pre-built funnels by adding new custom pages and existing pages or removing pages from any stage of the tube. You have complete influence there.

Are you looking to introduce a new product? You can create a five-page launch funnel with just a few clicks of your mouse, each with a different stage in the pipe, and they'll all be connected. The selection of pre-made funnels works for several niches and topics so you can find a tube that matches your particular needs.

Let's take a look at an example of a primary funnel from lead generation and the steps you can apply to that funnel to extend it.

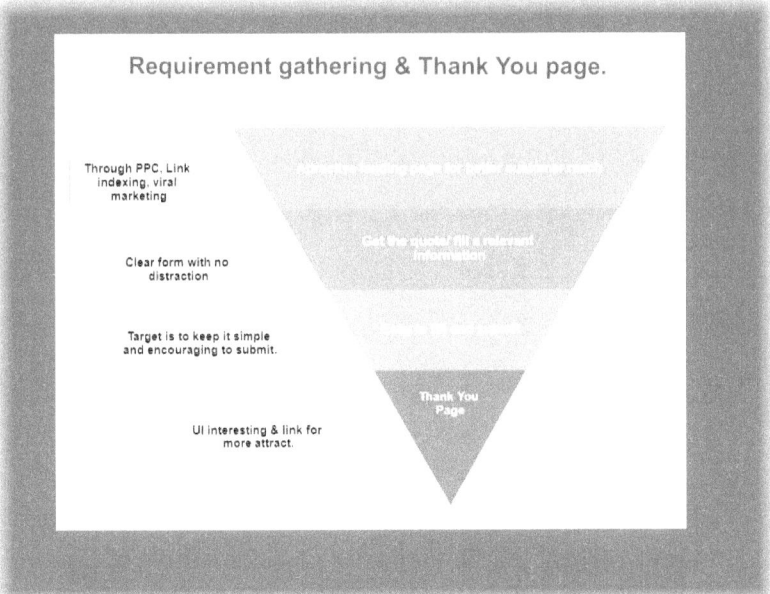

Optimization of your Wordpress website

Optimize database and images

Optimizing is a task, action, and procedure of creating something as fully working or productive as possible accurately. The main aim of optimization is to accomplish the best design or system, and these involve capacity, strength, and productiveness.

Why optimize the WordPress database?

It is a necessary procedure to sustain and optimize the WordPress database, and it should not reduce.

Take a backup of your WordPress database·before move forward and make sure that the backup of your WordPress database is running. Edit the config.php file after you make the backup to use the backup of your WordPress database and check everything works well.

How to Use WP-Optimize to clear up Your Database?

Before following any steps, make sure to produce a full backup of your WordPress install.

Install and start the WP-Optimize plugin from the WP Repository because it's accessible free from there.

Now for the plugin, you will have a menu item, so to open its dashboard, click on 'WP-Optimize' and click 'Database' or check data on separate tables. And you will also see the current size of your WordPress database when you scroll down.

At the top of the screen, you can also navigate the quick access menu to the different segments of this plugin.

Optimizing WordPress Tables

The primary thing is to checkout for is the choice to 'Optimized at a base tables '.This plugin can't optimize InnoDB tables, so you have to look over a box to overrule this setting. The purpose that you asked to do this is that if you are using an older version of MySQL, the optimization process will reconstruct InnoDB tables. Still, this circumstance differs from oneholdingprovidertoanother.Youcanselectinthemiddleofsafe optimizationsandtheones presenting an exclamation mark; this optimization brings the highest risk potential.

The highest risk potential optimization goes wrong is running; these optimizations could expand the burden on your server and generate it to reboot. If all this occurs, your database will be damaged.

But by choosing other optimizations, you can run them whenever you want and click 'Run Optimization'.

These are the other optimization you can run:

- **Clean all auto-draft posts** – Edited revisions of pages that never utilized but have saved automatically.
- **Remove spam and trashed comments** – All those deleted comments are still there, so removed them to save memory.
- **Clean all trashed posts** – Posts that are not removed even after 30 days in the trash, which can happen.
- **Optimize database tables** – Database contains multiple tables, and each table holds garbage and unnecessary data.
- **Clean all post revisions** – These contain the older versions of posts.

- **Removed unapproved comments** – Utilize this to remove all unapproved comments.

For proper learning, moving across all these optimizations and checking them one at a time, and after running an optimization, also check that your site still answers as you had expected.

Image Optimization

Image Optimization is an other excellent characteristic to help optimize your site, and for database, size has an indirect benefit.

Any other currently use image compression plugin can be replaced by this feature.

When one plugin performs multiple tasks, so there is no need for two active plugins. You can then deactivate and remove that one plugin that you don't want and giving up space inside your database.

When you turn on 'Automatically compress newly-added images', Image optimization is automatic.

And on each image, you can also select what level of compression to use:

- **Prioritize maximum compression**–the size of the file is small, and the quality of the image is lowest.
- **Prioritize attention to detail** – the size of the file is more significant, and the image quality is higher.
- **Custom** – To select the desired compression level, use a slider.

If you are not happy with the sizes of the image file you get, so you can adjust the plugin defaults to 'Custom' with the slider set in the middle.

Currently utilized to shrink your images, you will find the compression service under 'Advanced options'. So any of the default settings can't be changed.

On our sites, we only use Short Pixel with the above image optimization features. To bring it for a test drive, you can even get a free ShortPixel account, and it's fast, affordable, and as well as beneficial.

7.2   Improving monitoring performance

The basic definition of monitoring is that; it is a process of regularly keeping a record of a particular project or program. Monitoring is necessary because we have to know how much progress we have made and how the performance of a specific product is. Monitoring a website means to examine and verify that the users of that website can interact with it as per the expectations.

Monitoring a site is essential because it tells us about the performance, the functionalities, how much time it takes to load, and the increase or decrease in the website traffic. However, if you are using WordPress, then monitoring is quite simple as there are various plugins to assist you in monitoring your site.

Types of monitoring:

There are two types of monitoring. Let us discuss them one by one.

1. Synthetic Monitoring

Synthetic monitoring is the monitoring process performed with the help of a web browser simulations of the actions that the end-user may use on the website created through behavioral scripts.

Synthetic monitoring helps you to:

- Determine third party problems, if any.
- Determine the performance of the website during low and high traffic.
- Determine situations when your website or application can go down.
- Determines how the website will get responses across various countries.
-

Advantages of Synthetic Monitoring:

- Monitoring available 24*7.
- Determines the errors, if any and can fix them before it reaches the users.
- Monitoring performed from the end-users point of view.

Limitations of Synthetic Monitoring:

- Do not resolve any issues registered by the end-users in real-time.
- It cannot troubleshoot the device's incompatibility to use the application.
- It cannot depend entirely on the results produced as the monitoring is not performed on real traffic.

2. **Passive Monitoring**

Passive monitoring is the monitoring process that collects real user data and analyses its performance for a specific period. Passive monitoring provides more provides fully report of the website's performance.

Advantages of Passive Monitoring:

- It analyses real traffic.
- It gives an overview of the website's performance by real end-users.
- It provides proper communication between monitoring person and end-user to detect and solve any errors.

Limitations of Passive Monitoring:

- It requires more time to collect more data.

- It only determines how the website is working in existing conditions.
- Cannot monitor 24*7.

While monitoring your website, you need to keep in mind these three points to follow:

- **Uptime**

Uptime is a time for which a website is visible to the user. The uptime for your website should be 100% or close to 100%. Uptime monitoring also tells you that when your site is unavailable to users, you can take proper measures to handle that. When a website's availability goes down, then it is known as downtime.

- **Traffic statistics**

You can find out how many visitors have visited your website or, in simple words, what is the strength of the traffic your site is hosting. Traffic monitoring also updates you about the pages that are visited by the users.

- **Website speed**

With the help of speed monitoring, you know how much time it takes to load your website, the pages so that you can take appropriate action if needed.

WordPress is the most widely used platform to create websites these days. It is due to its easy-to-go interface and various features to improve its website quality. WordPress comes with different tools and plugins that help you monitor your website's performance in real-time. Let's see some of the best plugins that WordPress offers you to track your website.

- **Jetpack**

Jetpack is a free multipurpose plugin that was developed by WordPress to enhance the performance and functionality of your website. Jetpack includes many components that offer real-time monitoring. You need to install the jetpack plugin and configure it in plugin settings. Enter your email address so that you receive monitoring reports via emails. Jetpack monitors your uptime, downtime, visitors, speed of your website.

- **Uptime Robot**

Uptime robot is a freemium plugin that offers monitoring services for our website. You need to install and configure API so that you can connect it to your site. It is free for essential monitoring services, but for advanced options, you need to get the paid version.

- **Manage WP**

It is another free plugin that monitors your uptime, downtime, website performance, and security checks. You can set SMS alerts for the reports if you have a premium version of Manage WP.

Other than these, you can also use the external plugin for monitoring your website like:

- **Site 24*7**

Site 24*7 can track your mobile applications, servers, and websites hosted by WordPress. The basic version of site 24*7 that can monitor five websites is free, but to control more websites, you need to get a paid version.

- **Pingdom**

This application can monitor your website's status for multiple locations. The premium version gives you a feature of double-checking the faults and then sending alerts.

Optimization of your Wordpress website

Getting started with SEO by Yoast

When it comes to increasing the reach of the blog post or webpages that you created, it depends on search engines like google, yahoo, bing, etc.

Many webpages around the world would make sure that when people search about the content/service that you provide will land to your website. For that, you need to optimize your website's content like title, meta tag, text, etc. so that it pops up in the first ten search results of the content-specific searches. The process of optimizing content so that our website will rank 10 in search results for content-specific searches is known as Search Engine Optimization (SEO).

For a non-technical person handling all of these can be tedious, and they might have to compromise their content to optimize it for search engines. To handle all of those tedious tasks, so that you can focus on delivering quality content for your user, we will introduce you to Yoast, a WordPress plugin.

What is Yoast

Yoast is all in one solution when it comes to SEO. It will automatically handle all types of optimization in the website or manually if you don't want to depend on behind the scenes of an automated version. As SEO is a vast topic to cover and Yoast a plethora of manual changes required for SEO, it is not possible to cover every aspect of optimization.

In this topic, we will cover the surface of Yoast settings and features that will help you to get started with it. You won't have to face difficulty while learning advanced settings or optimization.

Starting with Yoast

First of all, you need to install Yoast in your WordPress. The installation process is similar to that of installing any other plugin or extension in WordPress. You can either search Yoast in the plugin section of your WordPress profile or go to Yoast official webpage, download a zip folder of premium version or free version and then upload downloaded zip the folder in the plugin section of your profile.

Once you have installed Yoast SEO plugin, you will have a notification in Yoast SEO > General.

Dashboard. "The configuration wizard helps you to configure your site to have the optimal SEO settings easily.

We have detected that you have not finished this wizard yet, so we recommend you to start the configuration wizard to configure your SEO.," and there will be a link in the message that will redirect you to Yoast SEO configuration wizard. If this is not your first time in Yoast SEO, you will have "Want to make sure your Yoast SEO settings are still OK? Open the configuration wizard again to validate them." in a notification message with a link that will redirect you to your Yoast SEO configuration wizard.

In the Yoast SEO configuration wizard, you would be to go through several steps, and depending on your answer to the questions asked in those steps, this wizard will complete the plugin's general settings. The items that will be in each step in the Yoast SEO configuration wizard is:

- Is your site ready to be indexed?
- What kind of site do you have? Like a blog, a news channel, an online shop, etc.
- Is it you or an organization? And some details about yourselves or organization depending on the option you chose.
- To show or not show posts and pages.
- How many people are publishing content on your site?
- Questions about your title settings.

The two questions asked in the next two steps in the wizard not mentioned above because that question is to introduce you to all the fantastic features of the Yoast. Those two questions are:

- Do you want to continue learning about SEO through our newsletter?

In simple words, they help you get familiar with SEO to get your site a better reach and update you about changes in search engines and Yoast settings or features.

- This step will have a success note with a link to a free Yoast SEO plugin training course.

Now you have completed your general settings; you need to optimize your content for SEO while you are writing that content. To do this, you have Yoast SEO meta box; this will help you write content that is both readable to your visitor and optimized for varieties of search engines. You will find Yoast SEO meta box at the bottom of your content in your editor.

If you are using block editor and don't find meta box there, you might have disabled meta box in search appearance setting to make it visible go-to SEO >, search appearance > taxonomies, then toggle the switch to show the meta box.

You can navigate through SEO by Yoast steps as follows:

1. Choose the correct focus keyword and write in the "focus keyphrase field".

2. Edit snippet for entering seo title, slug, and meta description which will change the article from yellow to green signal and can be published easily.

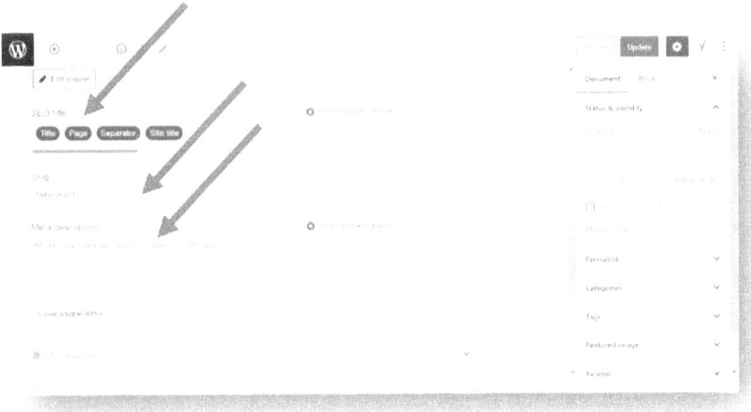

In the meta box tab, you will have options to analyze and preview your content, how your page will appear in a search result. Now let's discuss some of the analysis and preview.

Readability Analysis:

This analysis will help you to make your content more readable to your visitor or users. This analysis will give you feedback about your content as follows:

- **Score:** Based on the efforts needed to read your content, it will score your content. If you are writing for more educated visitors, then the score will be low.
- **Use passive voice:** This allows 10% of passive voice in the analysis as it's not possible to write without using passive voice and active voice, which makes the content more readable.
- **Subheading distribution:** This analyzes how you have organized your content. A properly-organized content helps users to scan your page faster.
- **Consecutive sentences:** This analyses the flow of the material.

- **Subheading distribution:** This analyzes how you have organized your content. A properly-organized content helps users to scan your page faster.
- **Paragraph Length:** As long paragraph in online content is not suitable as the reader doesn't prefer to read long and continuous content. So, this analysis tells you that you have used proper paragraph length in your content.
- **Sentence Length:** This analyzes sentences in your content, considering 20 words per sentence as a target length. Shorter sentences are much easier to read online.
- **Transition Words:** This helps to improve the flow of your content.

Snippet Preview:

In this preview, you will get to see how your webpage will appear in search results. You will also have options to edit snippets at the bottom of the piece and preview the piece in different screens like smartphones, tablets, desktops, etc.

SEO analysis:

In this optimization, you will add key phrases to your content and analyze your content according to key phrases. Here key phrase doesn't guarantee that your page will rank under Ten or under five in a search result for that key phrase. It only helps you optimize your content for that key phrase.

In the Yoast SEO analysis, you will get the following type of feedback as an analysis:

- **Keyphrase in subheading:** Adding key phrase in subtitle will make the importance of crucial phrase clear to search engines.

- **Key phrase distribution:** Improper distributed vital phrases will make your content weird and less occurrence will not be enough, so proper balance is required.

- **Image alt attributes:** This gives an idea to search engine about what this image is.

- **Outbound links:** If your site linked to other webpages, it will help search engines to relate your content.

- **Internal links:** It sets a proper structure to your site and helps search engines to suggest an appropriate part required to the user.

- **Keyphrase in the introduction:** Keyphrase in the presentation will clear right from the start about the page.

- **Keyphrase length:** The shorter key phrase is competitive, while longer is harder to optimize.

- **Keyphrase in meta description:** This is the first thing that the search engine looks for while indexing your page.

- **Previously used keyphrase:** The key phrase is for one page, not for a whole website, so it is advisable to use a different key phrase for different pages.

- **Text length:** We advise you to write at least 300 words on the subject to make it recognizable to search engines.

- **Keyphrase in slug:** Writing your key phrase in URL make your site clear even out of context.

8.2 Tools for searching relevant keywords

A keyword or key phrase is a word or phrase that describes what your content is. In terms of Search Engine Optimization, a keyword is words or phrases in your web page that a search engine uses to decide whether your site contains the relatable content for that keyword or not. Then search-engine will rank your page according to their algorithm to produce a convincing result to the user.

In a website, the keyword considered text in heading tags, title tags, image or video alt attribute, meta description tag, etc. In the world of web, where billions of webpages built every day, and many contents are being generated in the form of videos and image, choosing a keyword that will easily describe your content, less competitive among search keyword (that means many webpages are already optimized for that word). Even after including it several times in your content doesn't make your content senseless, it will be a very hateful and tedious task for any non-professional.

There many WordPress plugins or general tools that will help you to decide keyword and key phrases for your webpage according to content so that you do not have to compromise your content quality for a keyword or key phrase.

How Tools Help You in Finding Keyword

When it comes to choosing keywords, we need first to analyze the content that we wrote, and then we need to find a specific keyword that will help search engines find our page and show it to the result for that particular search. Randomly adding content to your web, the page isn't useful when it comes to reachability. We need to choose a keyword or key phrase and stick to that only while posting high-quality content. So that when any search engines see that increased content and think that your page is active, then these things help search drivers to improve the ranking of your webpages for that specific keyword. There are many WordPress plugins or tools that will do precisely that, while you write content or trying to find a keyword or key phrase.

Various tools out there analyze your content and give feedback and keywords or key phrases according to your content; then, you need to change your content or choose keyphrase, which you will stick and continue adding high-quality content.

We should focus on some points while selecting critical phrases from the suggestions of the tools like the search volume of that particular key phrase and does that key phrase is appearing in search suggestion of search engines or not. Now let's take an example of some actual tools or WordPress plugins that are popular among the community.

- **Yoast SEO:** It is one of the best WordPress plugins for SEO out there; it has many features to optimize your site. It helps you in adding SEO titles and descriptions to each post and pages on your website. To search for or analyze keywords and key phrases, it has Yoast SEO analysis that will give feedback according to your content and the key phrase you chose to analyze. It provides feedback on points like a critical phrase in subheadings, key phrase distribution, key phrase length, a key phrase in the introduction, a key phrase in the meta description, previously used keyphrases, text period, a vital expression in the slug, image alt attribute, etc., these feedback points will act as a test result, now to get content that is both optimized for search engines and readable, you need to make some small changes in content or critical phrase or Both to improve the result.

It also generates an XML sitemap for your whole website that helps search engines to crawl your site and import your SEO data if you are using another SEO plugin. It also gives you an option to add Open Graph metadata and social media images to your articles.

- **SEO Press:** This is another simple to use and popular WordPress plugin out there in the market. It has a much easier installation process, just like any other WordPress plugins. It is comparable to all the top SEO

WordPress plugins that are present there in the market in terms of features and easy to use. It has all types of features that a user can expect from SEO. WordPress plugins like editing metadata, title, description, open graph support, image and content XML sitemap redirects, content analysis, google knowledge graph, generation of metadata for twitter card, google analytics tool, google suggestion, broken link checker, google analytics stats, google news sitemap, backlink tool and many more. It has every advanced feature that will come handy for a professional like advance search analysis. Considering the premium version price, it is much cheaper than other WordPress SEO plugins with a lot of similar features.

- **Rank Math:** It is one of the fastest-growing WordPress plugins in terms of the number of downloads and features. Its installation is much easier than other plugins since it practically configures itself, verifies your site setting, and recommends the best for it. Then, a step-by-step wizard in the plugin will help you complete all setup of your sites like SEO, social profiles, webmaster profiles, and other SEO settings. It is the most user-friendly WordPress plugin that allows you to optimize your website's content to rank it higher in search engines. Its setup wizard enables users to import data from other SEO plugins during the setup. It has a feature that will allow users to add meta title, description, Open Graph metadata to your web page, or blog posts. This plugin also allows us to generate an XML sitemap, connect Google Search Console, etc.

8.3   XML sitemap and Webmaster

When we build a website, we made it by connecting many webpages. When you start building a website even for your blog or small store or any general-purpose, you might have few pages in the start, connected one another serving almost the same purpose. Still, as time passes, your website will grow, and you will end up having a website with more than 10's or 100's of pages, then definitely all the pages will have very much different purposes. Now let's assume you have a website with more than 100 pages, and almost all pages serve a different purpose.

In this case, when any user searches for the service you provide on some of your pages, it's wise to give them the link to that particular page rather than giving them a link to your website's home page. For this, you need to provide details of all pages and its connection to other pages to search engines, here comes the sitemap, as the name suggests it maps your website. Now you think what is XML sitemap in the heading, it's just the name of the method how you can store sitemap. An XML sitemap is a method that documents the details of all pages and their connection.

As XML sitemap is used by an SEO analytics tool to optimize your site, in almost all plugins for SEO, you will have this feature. If you want to do it separately, you can do it by using other WordPress plugins or any outsider plugin to generate an XML sitemap. Let's take an example of Yoast an SEO tool which had XML sitemap feature integrated with it and xml-sitemaps.com a web application for making sitemap, tools to get a better understanding of how to get XML sitemap for your website:

1. Yoast SEO a WordPress plugin: Here, you won't be getting a separate doc file for the sitemap, but some features that will allow you to use the generated sitemap for optimization purposes also export to another plugin if needed. To access or view the site, you can follow the following features:

- Once you have installed Yoast, you need to click on the SEO menu in the dashboard of your WordPress profile and then to features > enable advanced settings pages.

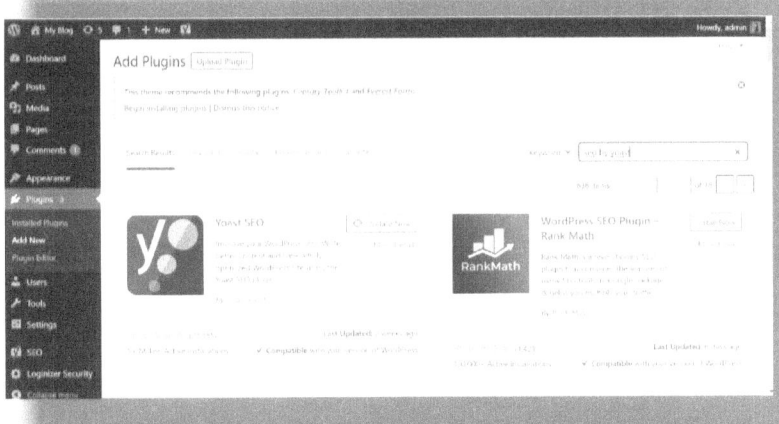

- Now you will see the XML sitemap menu in the dropdown of SEO menu where you need to enable XML sitemap functionality.
- After that, click on the "XML sitemap" link to see the XML sitemap.

2. Xml-sitemap.com, a web application: For accessing a sitemap, this method is much simpler than using an integrated XML sitemap feature, but for using it to analyze the website, this method is not that easy. To get the XML sitemap document, you need to enter the link of the website in the input field and click on the start. There is also a paid version if you want extra features like updating sitemap automatically, detecting and list broken links in your site, etc.

Webmaster

Building a full-fledged website can be tedious and boring, so we depend on many tools/plugins or services to complete the process of building a website. There are like 1000's of tools available in the market out there to do many different, simple, and small tasks essential to build a website. When a single tools or service do many tasks, we call it a webmaster. Like monitoring your site performance, identifying issues, submitting content for crawling, removing content that you don't want to be indexed, viewing the search queries that brought a visitor to one of the pages of your site, monitoring backlinks, etc. In simple words, the webmaster is a tool to analyze your website for performing better in search rankings. There are many tools or plugins to behave like a webmaster; depending on your requirement and affordability, you can choose which one you want to use. All of those plugins or tools have almost the same features and functionality. If you type "webmaster" in the search bar of the plugin section of your WordPress profile page, then you will get a lot of options like "SMNTCS google webmaster tool", "All in one webmaster", "analytics head", etc.

Here to explain to you the working of a webmaster, we will use a webmaster tool provided by Google, which is Google Search Console. Now, let's dive deep in, to get a feel of how to use a Google Search Console to optimize your site for better search rankings.

The Google Search Console or Google Webmaster Tool is entirely free. That have almost all of the features compared to other paid tools and provide a fantastic service by google to all webmaster (Here webmaster refers to a person who is professional in handling all functionality of a full-fledged website and analyzing it).

It doesn't mean that you need to be an expert to use it; it's effortless to use it. You don't even need to sign up for this you need to have a G-mail account, which most of you probably have. Login to your account and open the Google Search Console website, and you are useful to explore all the features of this tool and analyze your website. Giving an exact step by step guide on how to use it, is not possible because of the ever-changing user interface of the website to improve user experience and to add new features, but we can give you an overview of the tool. After all, let's have a quick look at how to use Google Search Console:

- Now you are on the website of Google Search Console; you need to put your URL or domain name (recently added feature) in the input field to get started.

- After giving a URL or domain name to the tool, you need to verify that you're the right person to have access to all the details of the website that you entered. That is to ensure the security of the website becauseGoogle Search Console allows you to update meta details and other site details for optimization.

- To verify the authority of the site, Google Search Console will give you three options.
    i.   HTML file: In this option, you have to download the HTML file and put it in the root folder. That is only possible when you have access to the folder in which you have your site or server where your website hosted. In many cases, you may not have those access.
    ii. HTML tag: In this option, you need to copy the meta tag given to you and paste it in the head section of your website's home page. In WordPress, you have plugins that give you the ability to add meta tags without editing the main

code of the home page. That is advisable because it poses some risk if you are just getting started.

iii. Google Analytics: In this option, you need to have a particular script tag in the head section of the home page of the website and the same google account in Google Search Console that you have used in google analytics of the website.

- Now that you have verified your website, you will access to all the features of Google Search Console and its analysis results.

Now let's discuss some features of Google Search Console that provide a quick glimpse of the activity of the website and analysis result of your website.

- In the dashboard, you will access all of your site's data, tweak the settings as you like, and read any unread messages you have.
- The visualization like Crawl Errors, Search Analytics, and Sitemaps will provide general site health and crawlability.

- In the settings section, you can have access to site settings where you can tweak the following two things.

i.   Preferred domain: It lets you choose what features of the domain you would like to have for your website, for instance, whether you want to index your site on search engine or not, how you would like to display the link in a search result.

ii. Crawl rate: It lets you choose how many times google should crawl your webpage.

- Change of address: This feature comes handy when you have migrated your website to a different domain or link.

There are many features and settings in the tool, but that will be a bit advanced to cover here.

8.4   Installing and configuring Google Analytics Plugin

Analytics, in simple, is a method that helps us to analyze the data that can be of any organization, institute, or a website. Google Analytics is a web service that was launched on 14th

November 2005 by Google that helps in tracking the traffic on your website and gives information on how users interact with your website and how they use it. It is easy to create a website with many different platforms today, and now, with the help of various plugins, we can also manage our sites. One such plugin which is necessary for your website is Google Analytics. So let's begin on how we can install and configure Google Analytics on our website.

1. Sign up for Google Analytics.

To create an account on Google Analytics, follow these steps.

- To connect your website to Google Analytics, you need to sign in first and create an account on Google Analytics.If you already have a Google account, then use it to sign in on Google Analytics, and then create a new google account.

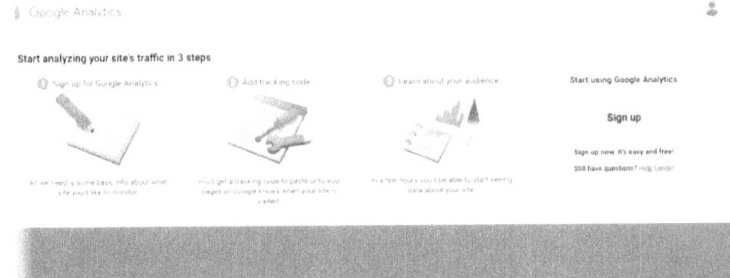

- When you have logged in to your google account, go to analytics and create signup, you will be redirected to another screen where you will see the following data.

- Go to sign up, and a page will open where you need to choose one from the two options: Web and Mobile. Choose Web.

- Next, you will be asked to enter the details like account name, website name, website URL, and the category of your website. Enter the details and click next.

- On the next page, you will be asked to accept the "Terms and Conditions." Accept them, and after you agree to terms and conditions, you will be given a tracking id. Copy this ID and save as we will need this ID in the future.

2. Adding Google Analytics to WordPress

We can use Google Analytics for WordPress. To do so, we can use any of the options given below.

- **Using a Custom Plugin.**

Here you can manually add your tracking id to your website. It is easy to create a plugin. You first need to check that the theme you are using has a wp_head in the header.php file. It is included by default, so not necessary to check.

Now create a new PHP file in an editor. You can name the file with your choice and paste the following code:

```
functionns_google_analytics() { ?>
<script                                   async
src="https://www.googletagmanager.com/gtag/js?id=
UA-XXXXXXXXX-Y"></script>
<script>
window.dataLayer = window.dataLayer || [];
```

```
functiongtag(){dataLayer.push(arguments);}

gtag('js', new Date());

gtag('config', UA-XXXXXXXXX-Y');

</script>

<?php

}

add_action( 'wp_head', 'ns_google_analytics', 10 );
```

Once you have finished, save the file and upload it to your site plugin folder WordPress-content → Plugins. Once uploaded, activate it as you activate it like any other plugin.

- **Installing a Plugin**

It is one of the easiest ways to add Google Analytics to your WordPress. MonsterInsight is the most popular WordPress plugin to add Google Analytics to your website.

Follow these steps to add it to your website.

i. **Install the plugin**

To install the plugin, go to plugin select Add New. In the search bar search for MonsterInsight. Once you find select

"Install now." After it is installed, hit activate. MonsterInsight is free, as well as premium. You can use a free version and access more advanced features like tracking of E-Commerce, Ads, Author, etc.

ii. **Connect to Google Analytics**

- When you activate the plugin, you will see a new menu on the screen named "Insights" on the admin menu. Selecting this will take you to a setup wizard for MonsterInsight. There at first, you will be asked to choose a category of your website that is a blog, business website, or an online store. After selecting the desired options, click on "Save and Continue."

- Now you will see an option "connect MonsterInsight" select that. This will take you to Google Analytics. Now you need to sign in. After login in, you will be asked to permit your WordPress plugin to access the data. Click on the "Allow" button.

- At last, you will be asked to select the profile you want to track. Select the website you want to follow. Finally, click on "complete authentication."

- After clicking this, MonsterInsight will install Google Analytics to your WordPress.

You can also add your tracking id manually. For this select "click here to authenticate manually" and paste your tracking id there.

Configuring the Google Analytics Plugin

You can also customize your plugin in terms of how the application works for you. Let's see what customization we can do when using the free version of MonsterInsight.

- Permissions

This feature allows you to change settings like displaying information, whether to auto-update or not, tracking usage.

- Engagements

This feature helps you to enable tracking of events on your website.

They have many other features, but they are only available when you get the premium version of MonsterInsight.

After Installation of the MonsterInsight plugin, you can select the settings as per your requirements. In most cases, the default settings work well. But still, you want more advanced features in your tracking just upgrade to premium membership of MonsterInsight and enjoy all advanced tracking features for your website like

- **File Download Tracking:**

shows you which files are downloaded the most from your website.

- **Outbound Link Tracking:**

Shows how many outbound sites you are sending your users to. It helps you to discover partnership opportunities.

- **Forms Tracking:**

Tracks the forms and gets you essential information.

- **Scroll Tracking**:

It helps you discover what content users are skipping at your website. It helps to see unwanted content on your website.

- **SEO Score Tracking**:

Tracks the statics of your SEO and helps you how to improve your traffic.

- **Post Type Tracking**:

Tracks how many audiences react to which post the most.

- **Author Tacking**:

Track the authors who visit your website most frequently. Helpful in blogs that have multiple authors.

The main advantage of using this plugin is that you can see your analytics data directly to your WordPress Dashboard. Just go to Insights and select reports.

There are many more plugins that you can use for your website in WordPress. Many of them are listed below:

- ExactMetrics
- Analytify
- Wp Statistics
- Enhanced Ecommerece Google Analytics plugin
- Google Analytics by 10web

Using Headers and Footers Plugin

It's another way to add Google Analytics to your website but not much advanced. We can't use this plugin for superior tracking. Also, this plugin does not allow you to view your dashboard statics as in MonsterInsight. To install this, go to plugin and search for the Headers and footers plugin. Install it and activate it.

After installing, go to settings and select Headers and Footers page. On this page, you need to paste the Google Analytics code. At last, click Save and continue.

Now you are familiar with how you can install the Google Analytics plugin to your website. There are many more ways to add Google Analytics to your website, but the easiest way is to use a plugin from the one discussed above.

SEO and Social Media Optimization

SEO

Before getting started, let's see what optimization is? The basic definition of optimization is to bring the best out of something. So, now we get an idea about what SEO is. SEO, commonly known as Search Engine Optimization.

It is a technique that helps you to increase the traffic in terms of quality and quantity on your website. In other words, SEO is a process that includes modifying your website's content to make it more attractive and visible to search engines. Many organizations, with the help of SEO, manage to stay at high ranks among different websites.

If your SEOis right, then your site will be displayed among the top websites. The search engine checks numerous websites and brings the best one out of millions of websites to showcase the best and proper content to its visitors. So, how does the search engine do this for us? The answer is SEO. The one with the best SEO rank is displayed first and the one with the least position posted at last. The visitor will go through the first page of the search engine and not to the last one.

How does SEO Works, and can you increase your SEO ranking?

You can never be sure that what people will search specifically that can bring them to your website. Let's take an example to understand how does SEO works. Suppose that you own a blog or a website that gives information on various fashion trends. Before posting your content, follow the steps below to make sure your site has good SEO ranking:

- **Note down the best words that people may search for.**

Since people don't need to search for the words and phrases that exactly match the title of your content, so, you need to figure out different words or phrases that are similar to the content that people might use to search for your website.

For example, people may search for "best fashion trends in 2020" or "latest fashion styles" or maybe "different styles to dress up". There can be many other ways to search. So, you need to think about the words and phrases as much as you can so that you can include them in the tags for your website.

- **Use Unique words for adding tags.**

Tags are an essential part that helps in increasing the traffic to your website as tags set the flow for the similar content that people expect to get. So, the good your cards are good is the results and ranking of your website.

- **Designing the page layout.**

Keywords and tags are just a part of having good SEO results. You also got to work on the pages. The pages you are creating must be more specific and structured so that it will be easy for the visitors to find the desired content they are looking for.

The pages should be optimized and should only contain the required information. If you are using WordPress, then you should first download Yoast SEO. It is simple to use and needs no professional skills to work.

To optimize your page, use the following steps:

1. **Search Intent**

Search intent is the person's goal behind his search. There can mainly be three types of search intent:

i. Informational: Being more specific about the topic.
ii. Transactional: When they need to purchase something from a website.
iii. Navigational: Looking for a particular site.

2. Using a descriptive URL's

A URL is created for that page when you create a page and post it on your website. The URL should be descriptive and short. The advantage of this is that it contains the specific keyword that may hit users' search results.

3. Use of Meta Title and Descriptions.

Meta descriptions and titles are shown in the header of the site. They tell the search engine about the type of content the site is containing. You should be very careful when writing the meta description. It should contain keywords, tags, or phrases, and it should not be too short nor too long.

4. Use of proper Headings.

Headings help the visitors to understand the layout of the page. You should use the HTML format to write entries on your web page. For example:

H1: can be used for defining the title.

H2: the subtitle varies in size from H1.

H3: can be used to categories the heading.

- **Linking the website.**

Linking the websites from other websites also helps you to increase your SEO ranking. When a page receives several links, it gives a positive result to search engines, which can boost the traffic on your website. So it is said that you must link your website to other websites so that you appear in most of the searches. Linking helps in increasing relevance, popularity, the reputation of your website.

- **Make sure your website loads fast.**

All search engines and the users give priority to the web pages that respond fast. Even you have an optimized page, structured content, or well-defined meta tags, if your website does not load fast, no user will visit the site, and the search engine will not display the website in the top list of the search result.

You can use GTMetrix or Page Speed Insights applications to check how long it takes for your website to load. You can also get relevant information on how you can improve the loading speed for your website.

- **Make sure that your website is device friendly.**

Since 70% of the population uses mobiles to search, you should make sure that your website is supporting both mobile and computer types of searches. You can use a Mobile-friendly test tool by google to test whether your website supports mobile searches.

- **Creating a Sitemap.**

Creating a site map is always helpful for the users as well as for the search engine to understand how different pages are connected. A sitemap is nothing but an XML file that gives information about the number of pages on your website. If you are using WordPress, then the Yoast SEO will automatically generate the sitemap for your website.

- **Internal Linking between posts and pages.**

It is another way to optimize your search result. When you have different internals links between various posts and pages of your website, then you have high chances that the search engine will display your site among the important ones.

These were some of the steps following which you can optimize your web page, which can increase your SEO ranking. There are many more things that you can do to improve your SEO ranking if you go more in-depth and spend some resources.

Let's look at the benefits of SEO:

1. **Good User experience**

SEO leads to an excellent user experience, which leads to the high popularity of your website, which means you have significant traffic on your website.

2. **Excellent communication between user and search engine**

By use of keywords, meta descriptions, and URL's it becomes easy for search engines and users to understand what type of content your website is containing.

3. Improving the website's popularity

The use of keywords and tags helps a website increase visibility and gain more audience and popularity among top-rated sites.

4. Increased genuine traffic

With increased popularity, vast amounts of traffic can be obtained which search for the same service you are providing, which is very difficult.

9.2   SMO

SMO is a short form for Social Media Optimization. SMO is a process of advertising the product on various social media platforms to gain the product's popularity. In simple words, we can say that SMO is a digital marketing strategy which can be used to increase awareness about a new product launch, different service about the organization. It is one of the best methods to connect with a real audience and tell them about your product and services using different platforms.

Now the question comes what is the difference between SEO and SMO when both have the same goals that are to increase traffic and popularity. Well, the answer is quite simple. SEO is a large set of strategies that we can use to increase traffic on your website and improve its ranking, while SMO is a part of SEO.

Steps to improve your Social Media Optimization:
According to Joshua Berg, who is a leading advocate of SMO, defined a seven-step model that can improve your SMO:

- **Reputation:**

The primary step is to build a reputation for your product. Your status tells people how you will provide the service, and your state also defines the quality of your service. You need to keep in mind that the content you are sharing to social media platform is unique and not copied from others. It can damage the reputation of your product and yourself too.

- **Engagement:**

It is another way of developing relationships with your audience. It consists of likes, shares, comments, mentions, hashtags, and feedbacks. You can tell the users of your website to connect directly by creating an account on your website, or you can ask users to use their existing social media accounts.

- **Authority:**

Authority is how people react or respond to your product and services. You can use Google Authorship to display the profile in search engines.

- **Leadership:**

It is a quality to control the people according to you. In terms of SMO leadership is the quality of an individual that how he shares his content and in what areas he promotes them.

- **Social Networks:**

To promote your product or services socially, you need to have a vast social media network to gain traffic on your website, and o obtain that you should come up with quality products. It is quality and not quantity that attracts the audience. So, focus on quality.

- **Using Right Social Media platforms:**

You must focus and promote your product on the right platform and to authentic communities. In my opinion, google plus, LinkedIn are some of the right social media platforms to gain attention to your product.

- **Optimization:**

It is the most crucial factor that affects the most to your SMO. Your content that you advertise to different social media platforms to diverse audiences should be ordered appropriately and contain all necessary information. So that people find it easy to understand what services you are providing to them.

Some of the techniques you can include enhancing the optimization of your SMO are by using:

i.   Share buttons to allow the sharing of your services at the individual level.

ii. Providing social logins to let them give feedback, including comments.

Using the above steps, you can improve your SMO ranking and attract large traffic to your website. These were some of the steps following which you can optimize your social media content, which can increase your website's ranking. There are many more things that you can do to improve your SMO if you go more in-depth and spend some resources.

Let's discuss some of the benefits of using SMO:

- **Establishing Brand**

SMO directly affects the audience and generate traffic to your website through Social media platforms.

- **Improves SEO ranking**

With proper techniques and quality services, SMO can help you increase the SEO ranking of your website.

- **Low Cost**

It is less costly to advertise on social media platforms as compared to promoting your product manually by using traditional methods.

WordPress gives you numerous options for different plugins to enhance your SMO. These plugins help you to optimize your content better to get the right audience, likes, and shares for your website. Some of the WordPress plugins are:

i. **Photo dropper:** this plugin helps you to add Flickr pictures to your blog or website.

ii. **Slide share:** this allows you to add a video presentation to your website.

iii. **Enhanced Sociable:** this plugin lets you add shareable social media buttons to your website or blog.

Customizing the Woocommerce Theme

Setup and Installation of Woocomerce Theme

Looking to run an e-commerce website? Don't know how to create an e-commerce website? Here, you will get to know everything about how you can install and set up a plugin that will help you create an e-commerce platform for your website. Woocommerce is a widely used WordPress plugin that is used to create and sell your products and services on your website. It is a free customizable plugin that you can install and setup on your WordPress site. The additional features are also available that you can use by paying for them. Let's see how we can install and setup the Woocommerce theme for our website on WordPress.

- **Installing a Woocommerce Theme.**

To install a Woocommerce theme, you have two different ways. Let's discuss them one by one.

1. **Installing your theme using WordPress.**

This is the most convenient way to install your WordPress theme for your website. To install the theme, go to WordPress.com and login to your account.

Go to "Appearance" and select "Themes" after clicking on themes hit "ADD New" Button. There in the search bar, you can search for "WordPress Business Themes". After you get your search results, select the appropriate theme, and hit the download button.

After the theme gets downloaded, click on the "activate" button so that your theme gets activated.

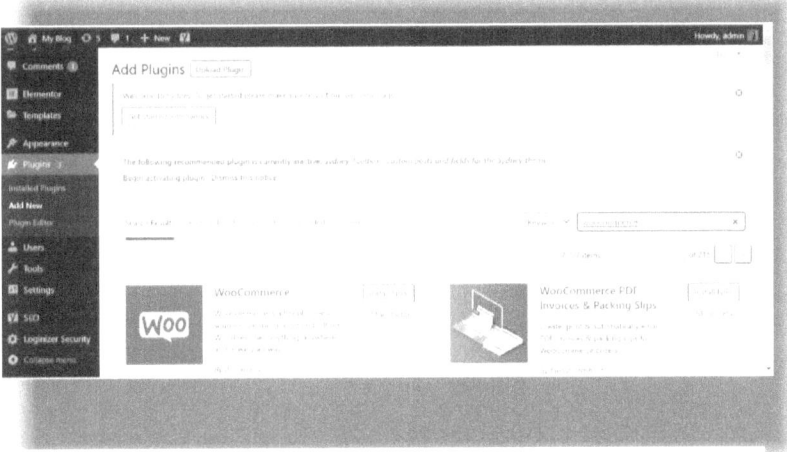

After the theme gets downloaded, click on the "activate" button so that your theme gets activated.

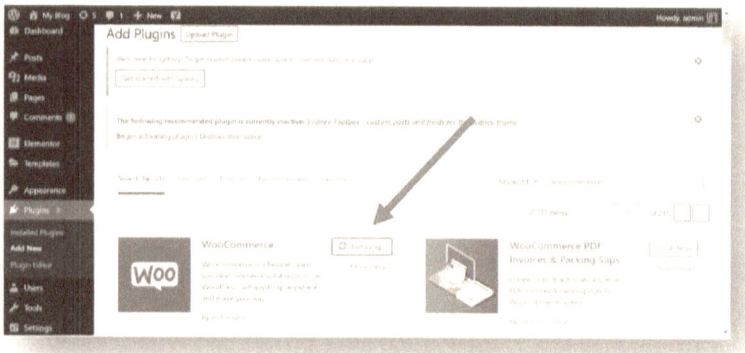

2.   Installing Theme from WordPress website.

It is the second way to download your WooCommerce theme to your site. To install your theme via this method, go to WordPress.org. The official website of WordPress will open, and there you need to select "Themes". After that, you will land on themes section of the website where you will some of the popular themes provided by WordPress on the screen.

Do not see the perfect theme that matches your requirements. Don't worry; you need to search for the theme in the search bar on the right side. You may search for "WordPress Theme for Business" or you can directly search for

"Woocommerce themes". Both options will show. You different types of themes. I suggest you go for searching "Woocommerce themes". This will give you the exact results. Now, you need to choose a theme that best fits your website. After you choose the theme, click the download button. You will see a zip file downloaded to your computer.

Now you need to upload the theme to your WordPress site that was downloaded on your computer. Follow the steps to upload the theme to your website:

i. Go to "appearance" on the left side on your dashboard.
ii. Select "themes".
iii. Click on the "Add New" button.
iv. Now select the "upload theme" option at the top.
v. Now a page will open where you will see the option to "Choose file". Click the option and select the file that was downloaded earlier. Wait until your file is downloaded. This may take a few minutes depending on the size of the file and speed of your internet connectivity.

vi.   After the theme file is uploaded successfully, click on install now to install and activate the theme.

The following were the two different ways that you can use to install the Woocommerce theme for your website. Some of the best rated Woocommerce themes are:

- Astra.
- Storefront.
- WooCart eCommerce.
- Ecommerce.
- eStore Pro.
- Divi.

Now let us discuss how we can set up the Woocommerce themes.

Setup the Woocommerce Theme

Since every time you download and install a theme, you don't get exactly what you need from that particular theme. You are often required to customize your theme according to your requirements. Let's discuss some points on how we can set up our new WooCommerce theme.

- **Installing Plugins**

When you install and activate a new theme, you are required to install some necessary plugins for your theme to run smoothly. Some themes contain the requirements in their documentations, while some notify you for the same. This may include sliders, banners, etc.

Go to your theme and select begin installing the plugin. You will see a list of plugins will appear in front of you on your screen. However, this may vary as different themes have different requirements, and you need to use them accordingly.

Just select the plugin that you find is useful for your website and install it and click activate the plugin to activate it on your theme. You can remove it afterward if you want to.

- **Customizing theme**

You can also customize your theme. To do this, go to "Appearance" and select "Customize," or you can also go to "Appearance" and then select "Themes" and click "Customize".

You will be landed on a new page where you can see several options on the left sidebar. The first is "Site identity," where you can customize the tagline and title of your site. Secondly, you will see a menu button here; you can customize menu functions like creating a menu, checkouts, cart, buttons, etc. You can also customize your front page in the "Front Page" section.

You can also add sliders to your websites. The colors of the menus and headers can be changed in the customization section. There is much more customization available that you can use on your site.

Customizing your website gives users a lot of flexibility so that they can easily look after and navigate to your website. You can add or remove the customization in the future that depends on your requirements.

The Theme will have few steps to get started- step 1

Step 2

Step 3

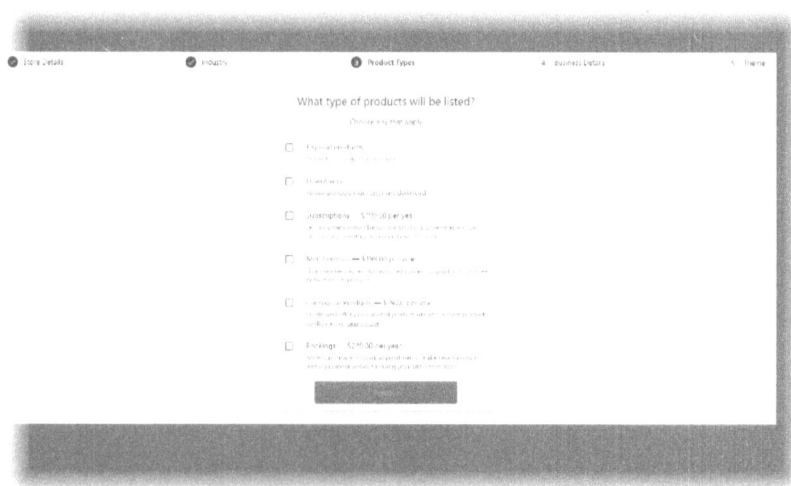

Step 4

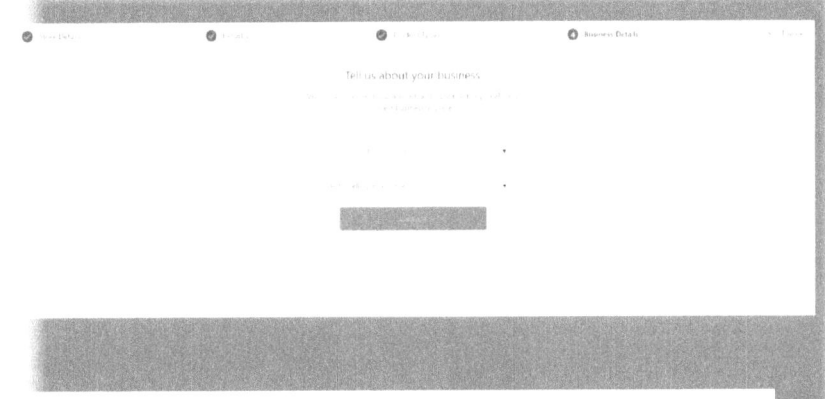

Step 5

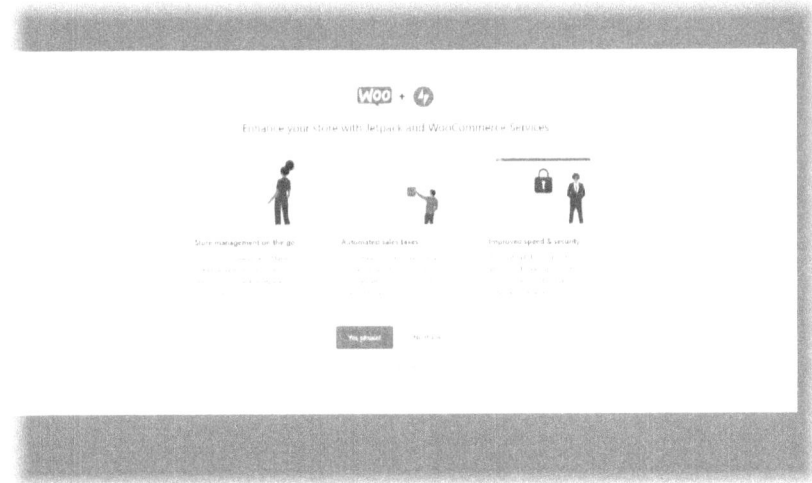

Step 6

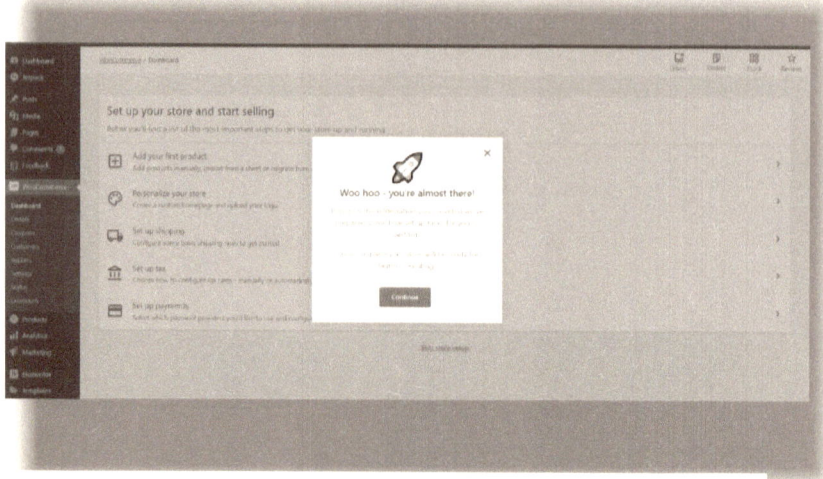

Step 7

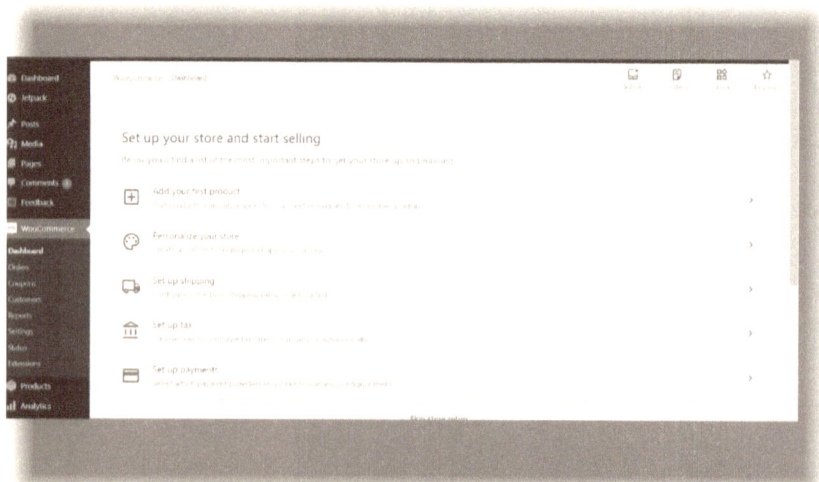

10.2   Adding products in WooCommerce

You are familiar with WooCommerce, and you know how you can install and setup WooCommerce for your website.

But it just steps one. Now you need to learn how to add products to your WooCommerce so that you can sell them on your website. Let's begin to learn how we can add products to our WooCommerce.

If you are running an eCommerce platform, you must know the different types of categories of the products. Well, if you don't know about them, let us discuss those categories first.

In the eCommerce world, you have six different products and all the products placed into those categories. Those categories are:

- **Simple Product.**

Simple products are those that have no sub-options available. They are only of a single type with no further variations—for example, a novel.

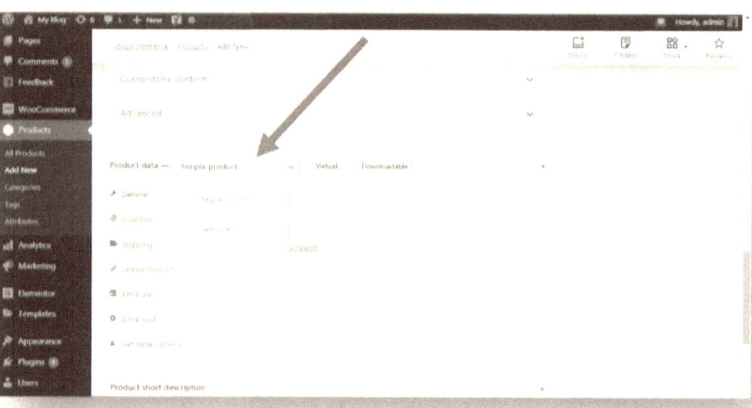

- **Grouped Product.**

Grouped products are a bunch of simple products that are grouped and sold out. For example, a bunch of five novels sold together.

- **Variable Products.**

Variables products are those who offer different variations of the product, like a mobile phone that comes with different specifications, colors.

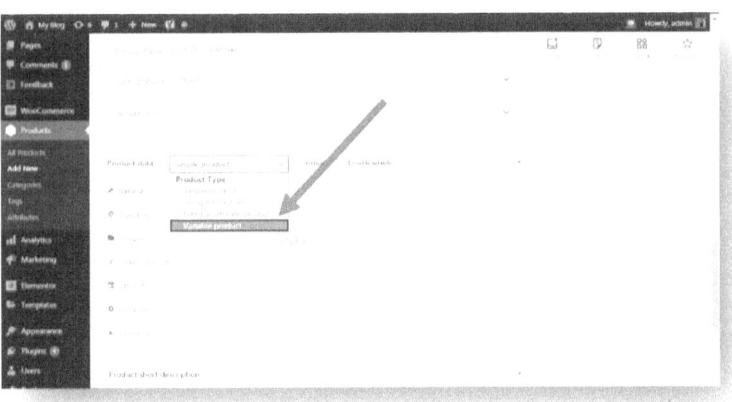

- **External or Affiliate Product.**

These products are sold externally but listed on your website. For example, you have merged all local vendors on your website. So the user buys it from your website but is shipped from one store in the area.

Along with this, there are two subcategories of the products available, which are:

1. **Virtual Product.**

These are the products that require no shipment and provide online services such as an online consultancy group.

2. **Downloadable Product.**

These are the products that are available by electrical means. Like, an eBook that you can download and read.

Now let's see how we can add products to our WooCommerce.

Adding a product to your WooCommerce.

Follow these steps to add products to WooCommerce.

i. Login to your WordPress account and go to Dashboard.

ii. Click on "WooCommerce".

iii. Then go to the "Products" section and there select "Add New".

iv. A new page will open, and at the top, select the "New" button and click on "product" from the drop-down list.

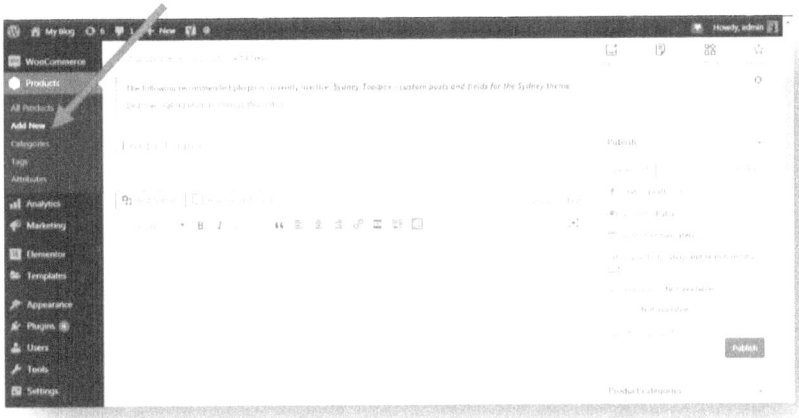

It was the first step in creating a product. Now in the next step, you need to add the details for your product. When you create a new product, you will be taken to the product page. This page consists of adding details of your product. Let us see them one by one.

- **Product Name.**

At the top, you will see a title bar that requires you to enter a new product name. Here you need to enter the name of your product. Keep in mind the name should not be too long.

- **Product Details.**

Below the title bar, you will see a text area where you can add the description about the product along which you also have a short description area where you can add a short description of your product, which will get displayed below the product.

- **Product Data.**

In this section, you will need to enter the data about your product type. In the first row, you will see the drop-down list in which you will find the product categories discussed above. Besides which you will see the option of the virtual and downloadable product also. Select them accordingly.

The product data section also consists of important information like the price of the product, sale price, etc. You can also schedule a sale duration by clicking the schedule button at the side of the sale section. You can also add taxes and tax classes for your product.

- **Inventory Section.**

You will see the "Inventory" option on the left side of your screen. Here you can manage the stock for your product. If you don't need this feature for your product, disable this in

WooCommerce settings under the product section, you will see inventory. Please select it and click on deselect. Manage the stock field.

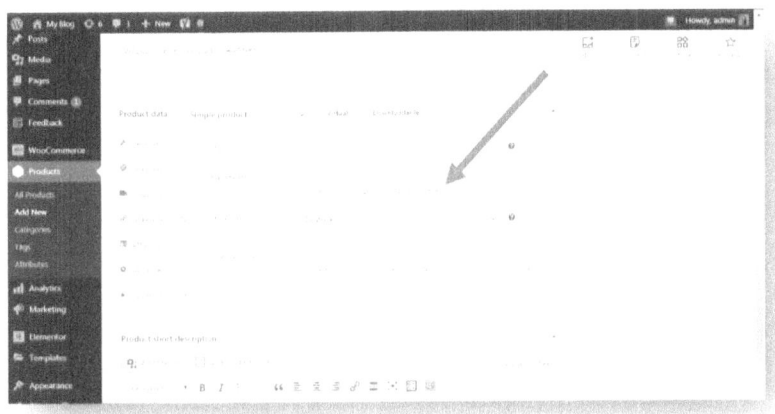

If you are managing the stock, you have the following option available.

i.   SKU, stock keeping unit that gives a unique code to each product in stock.

ii.   Manage stock, which lets you manage stock quantity, backorders.

iii.   Low stock threshold, that alerts you via email when the stock level reaches the entered figure.

- **Linked Tab section.**

Here you can link different products, either similar or different. It can help your visitor to choose from various products available.

Upsells

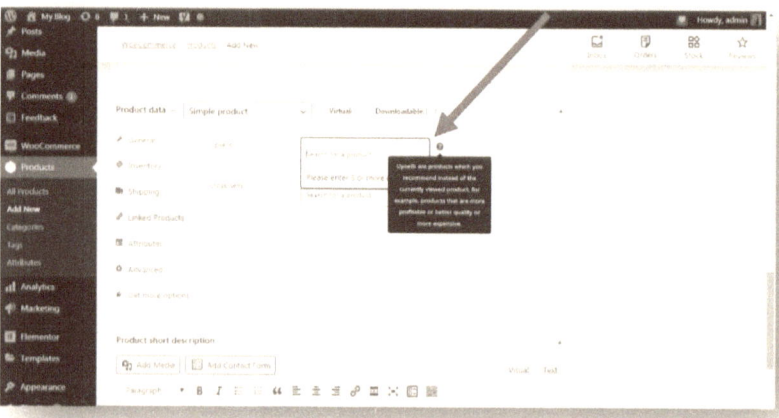

Cross- sells

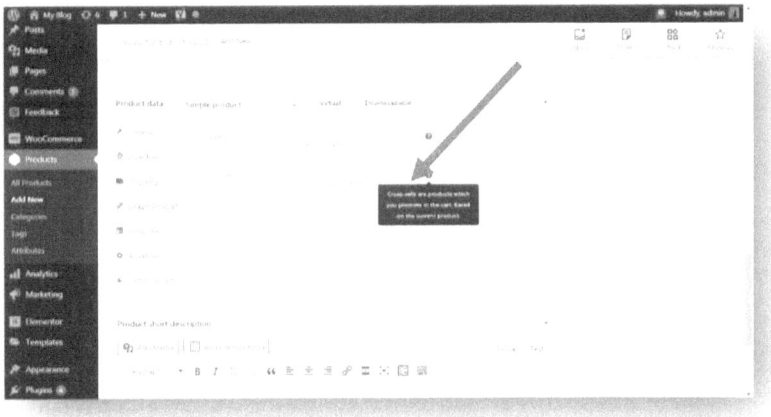

- **Adding product attributes.**

In this section, you can add attributes for your product. For example, if your product is a Shoe, you can add custom attributes like color, size. You can also choose default attributes.

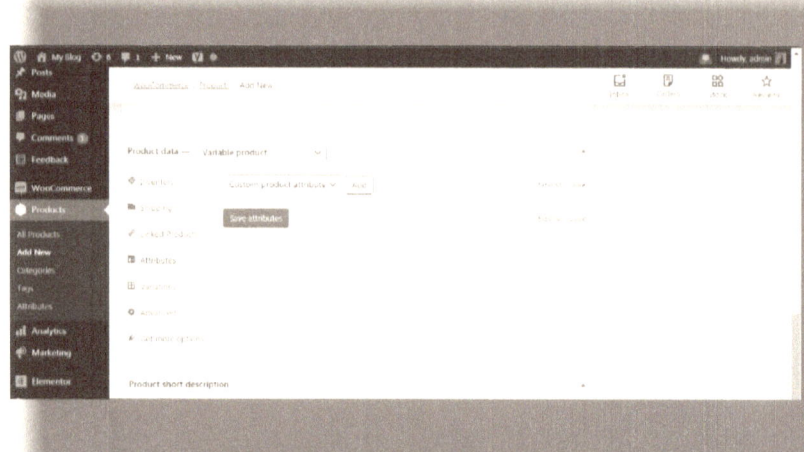

Create a new attribute:

Add-> name-> variable values-> Save attribute.

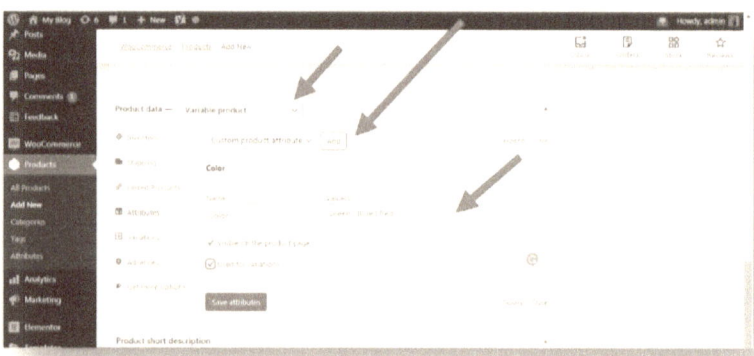

Add new attribute

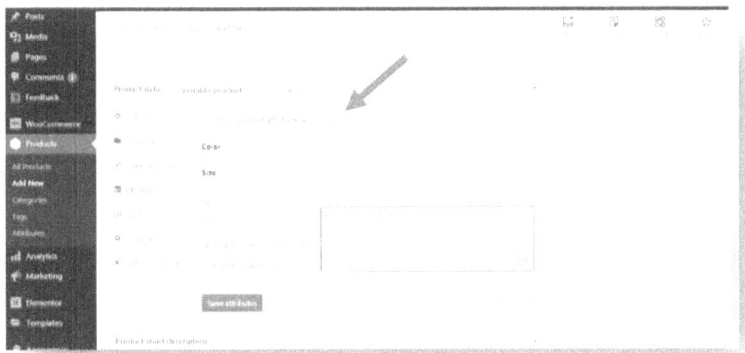

Select variations from left menu,

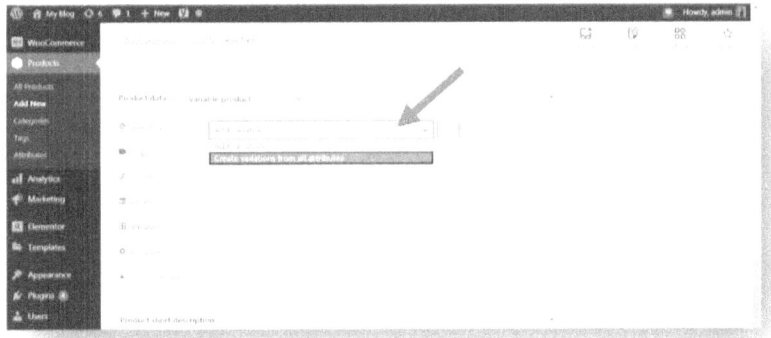

Once the second dropdown is selected, click on go tab. The popup will come to continue for creating variations. Selected yes and continue. Then on adding variations successfully it will again show a popup confirming that variations are added as given in below image.

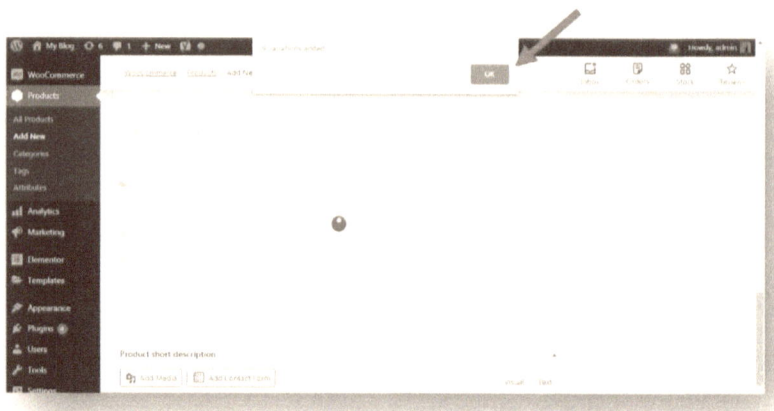

All the variations will come as shown in the below image. Now you can expand each variation and add details.

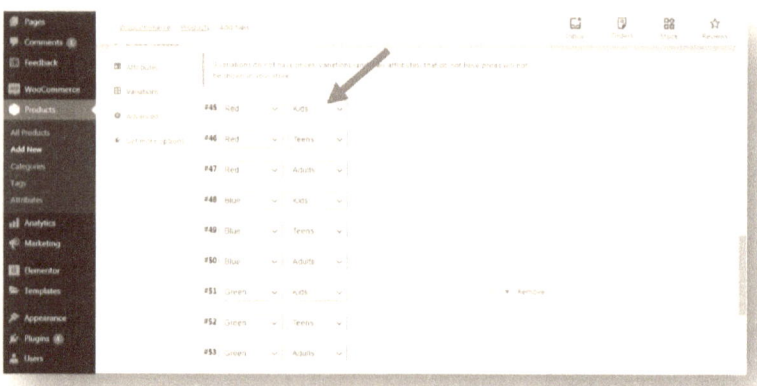

You can add all the details related to particular combination like, regular price, stock, weight, dimension, shipping class, etc.

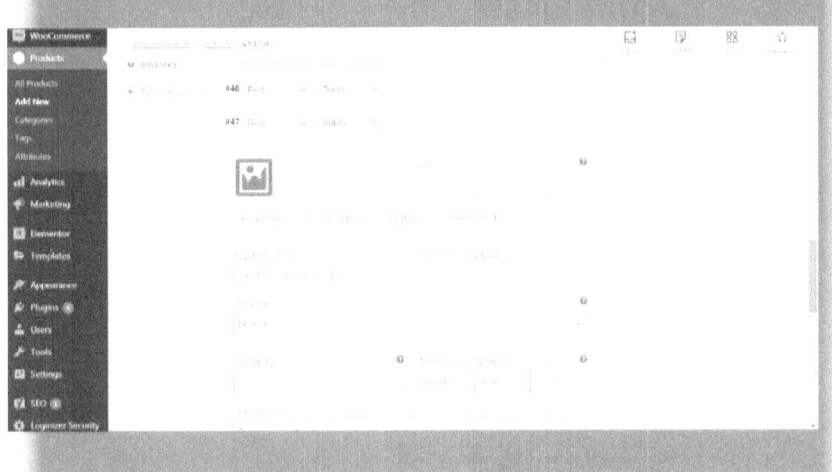

- **Finalizing your product.**

Here you can add an image for your product.

- **Publish the Product.**

After checking all the details you have entered, you are ready to publish the product. Hit the publish button to publish your product on your website.

Note: HSN code and price is mandatory. The weight also needs to be entered otherwise it will be

10.3 Installing Woocomerce Plugins and Extensions

We all are familiar with Woocommerce and its functions. It is a free open source platform that helps you to create a free online eCommerce store using WordPress. Woocommerce comes with a wide range of plugins. Let us see some of the most popular woocommerce plugins that can make your site better.

- **HubSpot.**

Want to track the activity of your customers, then HubSpot is made for you. This plugin tracks the movement of users. Another feature of this plugin is that it provides many free tools that assist you in marketing and sales services.

- **WooRewards.**

This is another popular plugin for your eCommerce site if you want to arrange rewards for your customers. This plugin allows you to organize a reward system when your customer purchases something.

You can choose a particular amount that the customer needs to pay to get the reward. The reward can be in the form of a coupon or cashback.

- **Woocommerce Product Zoom**

This plugin comes with the essential feature that allows you to zoom the product and give a more detailed version of it. This plugin helps you to zoom in and out when you hover your cursor over the image.

- **Woocommerce Gift Wrap plugin.**

If you wish to add gift wraps to your product, you can use the Gift Wrap plugin for Woocommerce. This plugin allows your customers to choose whether they need to add a gift wrap or not. You can add extra charge feature if the customer selects the gift wrap option.

- **Delivery date plugin.**

This plugin helps your customer to select a date on which they want their order to deliver. You can use this option during checkout.

- **Currency Switcher Plugin.**

If you run your website in different countries, you might provide the facility to your customers to switch currency. With the help of this plugin, the user can change the currency to see the price of the product in their preferred country.

- **Woocommerce Customizer.**

This is a plugin that is used to customize your Woocommerce website. You can modify buttons, text, labels, text fields. The drawback of this plugin is that you need to write PHP code to use filters.

There are many more plugins available for Woocommerce that can be used for different purposes. These plugins can be easily installed. After you installed Woocommerce, you can go to begin installing plugins section to install various plugins. Some of these plugins are free to use and comes with basic features, and you need to pay to use their premium features, whereas some plugins are not free and you need to buy them to use on your Woocommerce.

Installing a plugin is quite an easy task and is straight forward and can be done directly through your WordPress account while Woocommerce extensions are downloaded from Woocommerce.com and are installed slightly in a different way. These extensions are managed by the Woocommerce plugin only.

A Woocommerce extension is a small plugin that is used to extend the features of your Woocommerce plugin. While the Woocommerce plugins are available free of cost with basic features, the Woocommerce extensions are not free, and you need to pay for them annually to use them. If your subscription expires, you can still use the extensions, but you will not receive any updates after that till you renew your subscription. Let us see how we can install the Woocommerce extension.

Installing Woocommerce Extension.

To install and activate the Woocommerce extension, we first need to create a Woocommerce account on the Woocommerce website and connect our website to it.

Go to Woocommerce.com and create your account and then follow these steps mention below.

1. **Buy the extension from the Woocommerce website.**

After you have created your Woocommerce account and connected your website to it, go to your WordPress account and then go to Woocommerce.

2. **Connecting your site to Woocommerce.**

To connect your site to Woocommerce, log in to your WordPress. Then go to Woocommerce from the dashboard and select "Extensions" and click on Wooommerce.com.

There you will see the "connect" button, click on that. After that, you will see a dialogue box appears on your screen asking you permission to connect your site to Woocommerce. Click on the "allow" button.

3. Download the extension.

Now from the Woocommerce website, download the extension. This will be downloaded in a zip folder on your computer.

4. Upload and install the extension.

Now you need to upload and install the extension. To do this, go to Plugins and select "Add New" and click "upload". Search for the file on the computer and upload it. After that, select activate.

Your new extension is successfully uploaded, installed, and activated on your Woocommerce plugin and is ready to use.

To get updates and notification, you need to activate the extension the second time. For this, go to Woocommerce and then go to extensions and select Woocommerce.com. Now you can activate the extension. You can also activate the feature to auto-renew your subscription, depending on the feature provided by the extension.

Using the following ways, you can add and install extensions to your Woocommerce and make your website more flexible to your customers.

Some of the free Woocommerce extensions are:

- **Woocommerce tax**

It helps you to give live rates, taxes on your product.

- **Stripe**

It is used to accept all credit and debit cards for payments.

- **Square**

It is used to accept payments easily.

10.4 Woocommerce Tips

We are all familiar with Woocommerce, like how we can install it, add products to our Woocommerce, and manage our Woocommerce. Let us now discuss some of the tips that can make our eCommerce store better.

- **Using a Proper image for your product.**

Images tell everything about your product. It is the first thing that attracts the visitor. So, it would help if you kept in mind that the photos that you are using is well optimized and is of good quality. Also, your image should not take too long to load. It should load quickly.

- **Reviewing your product.**

Writing a review helps a lot to gain an audience. You must ask the buyers and visitors about their views for the particular product that they have purchased or are continually looking for. If you get negative reviews, you must work on the quality of the service or remove that particular product.

- **Make your products easily discoverable.**

Your products must be easily discovered so that the visitors need not search deeply to find the product they are looking for. To do this, you can divide your products into categories and sub-categories. Like for example, if your website sells mobile and clothes, you can types them into electronics and fashion by further dividing them into sub-categories like men and women fashion.

- **Describing your product.**

Your product description reveals everything about the product that you are selling. Try to describe your product uniquely and efficiently so that the buyer finds it easy to understand its features.

- **Zoom in and Zoom out feature in the image.**

You can use YITH WooCommerce zoom magnifier plugin to add zoom in and zoom out feature when the customer moves the cursor on and off from the image. This makes the image clearer and also makes your website look more professional.

- **Adding new products.**

It is mandatory to add new products and services at a regular interval of time. This will help your website to grow and gain more audience. It will also improve the quality of your website.

- **Choose a good interface theme.**

Your store should look catchy, and at the same time, it should have an easy to use interface. It is required that you should use the theme which has an easy to understand interface so that the user finds it easy to hover from one page to another.

- **Securing your data.**

It is the most essential to use the best securities option available for your site. You can use the various free and paid plugin to secure the data on your website. You can also install the SSL certificate to ensure your customer that you are using the best security measures to secure your data.

So, these are the few tips using which you can make your online store better. Many more tips are there using which you can make your WooCommerce look outstanding to your customers.

Monetization of WordPress Website

Tricks to drive traffic to your website

Creating a website is one thing. Maintaining a website is another challenge. You need to equip your website with the best features and easy to use interface. Your website is of no use until it hosts minimal or no traffic. It is no easy to gain traffic quickly by just creating a website. You need to have a highly optimized website to increase traffic. If your website is not optimized, the search engine will not show it to users at starting pages, and the users will not scroll down to the last search result to look for your website.

Besides, having a well-optimized site, it is not sure that visitors will go to your site. Many of us face this problem. So, to solve this problem, let us look for some tricks that can increase traffic on your website.

There are numerous tricks that you can use to attract traffic to your website. We will see some of the best ones.

- **Advertisement.**

It is an essential way of attracting people towards your website. Advertising directly tells people about the product and services you are providing to them. The goal of advertising is to gain people's attention towards your product with all the necessary information. Social media advertising is the most popular these days. You can use social media platforms like Facebook, Instagram, and LinkedIn to promote your product at a very reasonable cost. You can even hire an external advertising agency to promote your website at a higher cost.

- **SEO.**

This is another most essential factor that helps you to gain traffic on your website. SEO stands for search engine optimization. SEO helps you to enhance the quality of your website. Using SEO, you can optimize your site by defining a structural representation of content, meta description, and use of keywords. This helps increase your site rank so that it appears in the search engine's first few search results.

- **Creating a Backlink.**

A backlink is a link to your website from another website. In simple words, a backlink is a reference to your site from some other web source. You can create a backlink for your site by providing interlinking with your posts, or you can tell other bloggers or websites to promote your link, but in that case, you must have quality content on your site.

- **Guest Blogging.**

Guest blogging is the most widely used technique that helps you to gain traffic. Guest blogging involves writing posts and publishing them for other websites, and in turn, those websites link to your websites, so you get quality traffic.

- **Avoid the use of auto traffic generators.**

Many of us think that they could use external websites that generate traffic for your website. You think it is easy, and no one can recognize this spam activity. Well, you are wrong. Google keeps track of all the activity on your website. If Google detects that you are generating traffic by an unfair means, it may affect your reputation and ban your site. So, keep in mind that you do not use any such ways to generate traffic.

- **Google Maps Advertising.**

This is another way to attract traffic to your site. It is a paid yet more effective service offered by Google. With the help of google maps, you can list your brand location and help users reach you. This is a better option if you own a store and have a website for it.

- **Video Marketing.**

We will all know that the marketing of your product plays a vital role in generating traffic. Video marketing is a category of digital marketing where you help the user to understand your product and services via a short video.

It is the most effective form of marketing because the viewers get a better look at your product, and through a video presentation, it is easy for them to understand your product.

You can use social media platforms like Facebook, Instagram, or LinkedIn to promote your video. The video should be short and should contain only the necessary information related to your product.

- **Boost up your site.**

It is essential that your site loads quickly. Your site should not take too long to respond. The visitor does not like to wait, and they prefer websites that give the instant result on a single click. You must use online tools to check whether your site loads quickly or not.

- **Make your site device friendly.**

Since today the majority of the population uses their mobile phones to search the web, you must take care that your site should load quickly on any device that is used to search it. It should be able to load on your mobile phone as quickly as it loads on your computer.

- **Feedbacks and reviews.**

Many of us don't take reviews and feedback seriously. But this plays an essential role in gaining and maintain the traffic of your site. With proper feedback and reviews, you can know what your users want from you and whether they are happy with your services. You can also organize a question and answer session for your website, where you can allow your users to rate your site and give suggestions about how you can improve the quality of the service you provide.

You must take the feedback and reviews seriously and work on them so that you can improve the quality of your website, directly affecting the strength of the traffic on your website.

These were some of the techniques that can help you generate high-quality traffic on your site. There are many more such tips that you can follow to do the same. But it is the quality of your website that generates traffic. So, if you want to host lots of traffic on your site, then you must work on the quality of your content.

 Note: You can also start Facebook and Instagram ads campaign to get traffic on your

11.2 Interlinking and Backling

All website developers know what the role of SEO and how important it is to improve our website's rank is. SEO plays a vital role in maintaining the rank of your website as well as to gain traffic on your site. SEO uses strategies that directly affect your website's quality, which in turn results in gain or loss of traffic on the website. There many SEO strategies that you can perform on your website to optimize it. Today we are going to discuss two such SEO practices that will help you drive traffic on your website.

1. **Interlinking of Websites.**

Linking means connecting two or more things. In terms of SEO, interlinking is a process in which the current article/ post has a link to a previous article or post on your website using a hyperlink. So, when the reader clicks on that link, he is redirected to that particular post. This helps the reader to understand the concept and your topic better. Interlinking is only done within the same domain.

Interlinks help in organizing your website's architecture as interlinking helps connect the content of your website and tell Google or any other search engine about the structure of your site.

Advantages of using Interlink.

There are many advantages of interlinking, some of which are discussed below.

- **Increases the average time of users on your website.**

When a user reads an article on your site, and if those articles are interlinked to other articles, then the user may go through those links. This will increase the time spent by the user on your blog or website, which will increase the website's ranking.

Well, the topic's content should be proper and must be related to other articles so that the reader is curious to gain more knowledge about the subject.

- **Interlink provides link equity.**

Link equity, also known as "link juice" is ranking given to a website based on the internal links provided, topic, and many more things. The search engine uses link equity to determine the page rank.

- **It helps in improving the quality of your website.**

Internal link helps to build a strong SEO, and a strong SEO helps increase your website's quality. This will improve your website ranking, which means your website will appear in maximum searches.

2. **Backlinking of Websites.**

This is another SEO practice that helps you to improve the quality and ranking of your website. Like Interlink, a backlink is also a link with a difference that it connects two different websites. Yes, a backlink is a link that used to redirect the user to another website. It is one of the essential ranking factors for most of the search engines like Google because when a website refers to another website through a backlink, it means that website has valuable content.

There are two types of backlinks tags.

No-Follow Tag

When you use the no-follow tag, you tell the search engine to ignore such a Link in determining the site's ranking.

Do-Follow tag

When you use a do-follow tag, it means the site that you are referring to contains valuable content. Often this type of tags is taken into consideration while determining the site's ranking by the search engine.

Advantages of Backlinking.

- **Refers traffic.**

Creating a backlink helps to generate traffic on your website. This helps in improving the quality of your website as other websites refer to only quality websites. If a website is providing a link to your website, it means you have quality content.

- **It helps search engines to find your website quickly.**

If a website has a backlink to your website, then it becomes easier for a search engine to find your website. If your website is new, you need to get a backlink for your website so that it is discovered fast and crawled by search engine bots.

- **Builds your brand name.**

Backlink helps you to popularize your brand name. When a site creates a backlink to your website, it increases its value, and your site becomes popular. The number of backlinks directly affects your brand popularity. So, you should get backlinks as much as possible so that a broad audience visits your site.

11.3   Outbound Marketing Plan

To those people who desire to have business out from or a pre-built small network. All of you will need a proper marketing plan to grow your business. Depending on the types of products or services, your business provides to your customer. You need to plan a strategy to market your product or services. There are many ways you can classify or describe how to market your product or services. Here we will talk about outbound marketing, which works very well considering the situation, product, or service.

Outbound marketing is a plan in which you need to talk or spread awareness about your product or services to your customer. To understand what is outbound marketing lets talk about in inbound marketing. Inbound marketing is a strategy where you don't need to go to the customer to talk about your product and services. People in need will directly come to you for a solution like writing a blog and putting your services or product on a platform, whereas mailing to your customer about products and services is an example of outbound marketing. Both types of marketing are inbound; outbound has its benefits depending on the current scenario or where your business is lying in terms of growth.

Outbound marketing provides you linear growth, whereas inbound marketing provides you exponential growth. Consider writing a blog and mailing a customer about your product in the first case you have to wait while in another case you have a fair chance you will get your customer attention instantly. Now you have the fair idea about what outbound marketing is, let's discuss how to plan a strategy for outbound marketing in the following steps:

1. **Know your offerings**
2. **Know your audience**
3. **Research your competitors**
4. **Create a message campaign**

Let's discuss more on above key points:

1. Know your offerings:

Being part of the business, any way you know your company's offerings, but there is a subtle way you put your knowledge of your business as a marketer or owner. You should have a clear goal of what you want to achieve through your outbound marketing campaign. Like if you are building webpages, you need to explain the benefits if they have the webpage or different features you are providing, which is different from your competitors.

2. Know your audience

Since the audience plays an important role in the growth of your businesses, it is always better to know who your audience is and their preferences. You should research the habits, content preferences—consumption choices, etc. of your audience to plan your marketing strategies. For example, digital media services like video games should market their product on social media platforms; for video games, we have YouTube, Reddit, steam, etc.

3. Research your competitors

In outbound marketing, we market a product on different channels like bill boats, tv ads, flyers, etc. as all of these are very large numbers, so the probability that people will get attention to our product is very low. In a way, we can say that pretty much all potential market channels are saturated. To stand out, it is imperative to keep an eye on your competitors.

4. Create the message for a campaign

To make an image like branded products properly, you need a phrase that will be able to communicate with your customers on behalf of your companies/ firms. Make a list of messages you want to convey and frame it in a phrase or line or, if possible, in one slogan. Ideally, a campaign message consists of a campaign name, headline, slogan, and hashtags. The message should subtly convey the value or benefits consumers will get from your product or services, and it should be memorable enough for brand recall. Example KFC- its finger-licking good, coca-cola, McDonald's- I'm loving it.

11.4 Affiliate Program for Beginners to get Enrolled

Knowing how to market affiliates is critical to your success as an affiliate marketer. But even though you have beautifully set up your website, ad, or social media channel, you still need a trader to work with. It is here that affiliate programs bridge the gap.

You'll learn all you need to know about affiliate marketing programs in this post. You can see why they are necessary and learn more about some of the best services as a beginner open to you.

But first of all, you must know what they are and how they work.

Understanding Affiliate Programs

In concept, affiliate programs, also referred to as affiliate networks, are relatively simple. All they do is provide a platform for third parties, allowing merchants and affiliates to find and work with each other.

Afterward, merchants and associates will sign up for the website, find each other, and start working together.

But behind the scenes, these networks of affiliates are complex behemoths that do much more than help merchants and networks of affiliates. We also offer both parties some essential services.

- How many watch a banner ad
- How many people end up shopping
- How many clicks a source gets on an ad or blog
- Revenue generated by an affiliate and offered to multiple merchants

And that is just the iceberg tip.

Think about what would happen if no one tracked these data points. Affiliates would have a hard time getting paid, and affiliates presenting false results could rip off the merchants.

So, the affiliate services have their work cut out for them between developing relationships and monitoring the entire affiliate marketing cycle. It makes all the difference in the world when a program does a good job, though.

And most affiliate networks charge a commission for each completed action, in exchange for their services. It ensures free use of channels and offers you a great way to make a living as an affiliate marketer.

Best Affiliate Programs: Amazon Associates

The Amazon Associates are first on the program list.

Since 1996, Amazon Associates has laid the foundation for partner services. Indeed it was the world's first online marketing affiliate program.

Since its inception, affiliate marketers have been helping to raise money by appealing to the millions of consumers who shop annually on Amazon. If an Amazon partner shares a connection leading to a sale, referral fees received from the purchase.

And as thousands of companies are learning how to sell on Amazon every year, the potential for affiliates to grow is seemingly endless.

All you need to do to get started as an Amazon affiliate is click the Join Now for Free button on the Amazon Associates tab.

If you have an Amazon account already, you will be prompted to log in to get started. If you are not already on Amazon, first you will have to build an account with some basic details.

Once you see the classic progress bar on Amazon, you'll know you 're in the right place:

From here, you will be taken through a relatively detailed process that establishes your account with your Associates.

Next, you will be asked to tell Amazon what websites or devices you want to advertise on. If you have a blog or website of your own, you will be entering it. You will also be asked to share what your niche is, what you are hoping to sell, and how you plan to drive traffic and monetize.

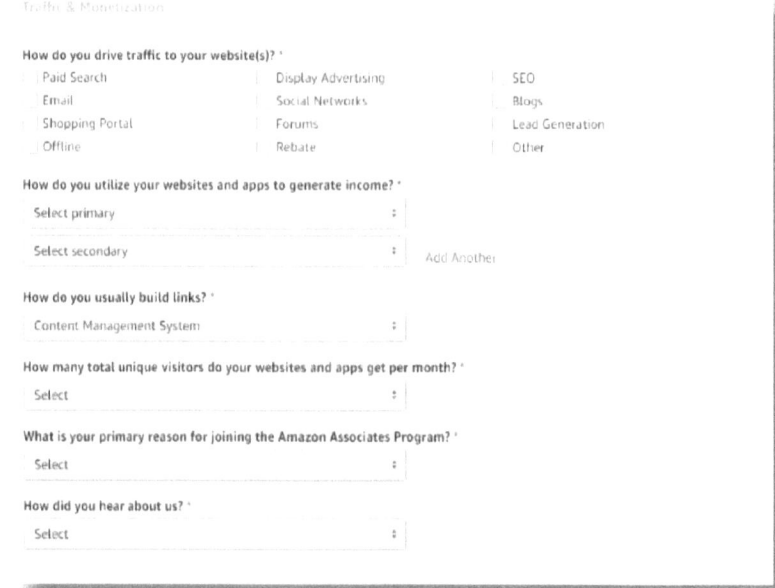

Once the application process is complete, the last step is just a quick verification of the security. Amazon prefers to call you, so make sure that your phone number is correct to proceed.

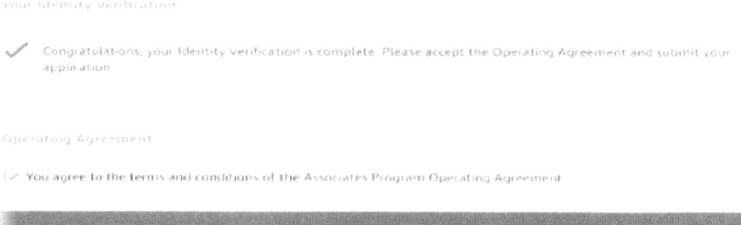

And last but not least, you will need to set up your payment and tax info with them at some point, so you can get paid. After all, you don't want to work for free and always have to pay your taxes.

At this point, as an affiliate, you are ready to start finding products to promote. And luckily, that is an extremely simple operation.

Start by finding the search bar for the product on your dashboard. And it looks like this:

You can insert words here, and check for things in your niche. Or, you can press the tab at the top right, and manually search objects.

Once you have started the search, you will be redirected to a page with simple results. Scroll through the products, find one you like, or start searching until you have found what you are looking for.

Once you have found the item you want to advertise, the last move you need to take is to click on the corresponding product in the yellow down arrow. This brings up your chosen product's text link, which you can use to share in your promotions.

Amazon Associates is a tried and true program that has created thousands of successful affiliate marketers. As Amazon's affiliate, you will be an essential part of the world 's biggest online retailer.

Here's a glance at the pros and cons to consider when determining if you want to become an Amazon affiliate:

Pros:

- Around 1.6 million products to choose from
- Sign up for free
- Trust in Amazon means selling is so much simpler
- Simple to customize links or advertisements
- Small thresholds for payout

Cons:

- Cookies last a mere 24 hours. Upon sales are not ascribed to you
- The commissions are low according to some criteria
- Challenging international payouts
- Paypal doesn't work

Affiliate Programs: ClickBank Affiliate

ClickBank is one of the most valuable resources for affiliates beginning to study which goods they would like to sell in their niche. It is a valuable tool because their information is entirely open to anyone without an account.

But ClickBank is more than a mere tool for research. It's also a fully functional affiliate program that can help you jump into affiliate marketing head-first.

ClickBank started a garage in 1998 but increased to become one of the world's top retail locations. They currently boast more than $3 billion in sales each year.

They 're an excellent option for affiliates because of their success and 20-year history, no matter what your expertise. They 're hard to pass up with tons of products to promote and a wide variety of merchants to partner with.

If you want to start earning money, you'll need to launch an account to become a ClickBank affiliate. Input your details and payment information, then finalize your account to get started.

You'll also be asked to complete a short survey to help ClickBank give you a better experience once the process is done.

The rest is relatively easy once you get through the setup. As a newly minted member of ClickBank, you will have a massive resource pool at your fingertips. This can help you find out more about what ClickBank has to offer and answer any lingering questions you may have.

Pros:

- The vast product range suits a wide variety of niches.
- There are several goods which have very high commission rates.
- Recurring commissions are promoted.
- Easy to use and simple procedure for generating links.
- Lots of resources to help you learn the ropes.

Cons:

- Large selection of products 'spammy' that wastes time and undermine credibility.
- A lot of rivalry for products of high value.

Affiliate Programs: eBay Affiliate

The eBay Partner Network is the meaning eBay provides to an affiliate system. They give affiliates the tools they need with as little fuss as possible to promote the eBay products. No matter how you choose to market products, you can make good use of eBay's affiliate program.

Unlike some of the other affiliate marketing programs in this chapter, you'll be working directly with eBay and its products as an eBay affiliate. Although you'll be working to support sellers to a small degree, the primary partnership is between you and eBay.

And just like Amazon, you 're going to work with a platform that companies want to sell on. Growth is pretty much guaranteed.

As a bonus, eBay doesn't require that you work exclusively with them. You can be an eBay affiliate and still work to make additional revenue with other merchants and programs.

You'll need to apply to join their affiliate program, which takes about five minutes to get started. It is one of the more natural processes of application, by far.

All you need to do is sign in to an existing account, or register with eBay to start a new account.

Sign in  Register

Email or username

Password

Sign in

✔ Stay signed in Text a temporary password

Reset your password

 Using a public or shared device? Uncheck to protect your account
Learn more

You will be asked to check a few pieces of information once you sign in with your account, pick your country of residence, and then you will be done. All you need to do now is find goods, build your affiliate connection, and start promoting them.

And, luckily, eBay is making you that simple. You have two main options for establishing your affiliate links, and they both take hardly any time.

First, you can browse eBay, copy the URL, and paste it into your eBay affiliate dashboard for a product that is in your niche.

You will then be given a link to your affiliate, which can be used in your content.

The second way is quicker, but you need to install a Bookmarklet icon in your Bookmarks Bar. That might sound confusing, but it's pretty easy.

All you need to do is find the icon in your eBay dashboard and drag it to your bookmarks bar afterward.

Pros

- Large product range with no limits to choose from.
- Commissions vary between 40% and 80%.
- Fast system of payment that works with PayPal.
- Links are incredibly easy to generate.

- Buy it Now buttons can shorten times of purchase.

Cons:

- Some buyers prefer purchasing fresh models, not used models, or by auctions.
- Auctions also last longer than partner cookies, but you are not paid.
- Selling platforms on eBay can be frustrating, and customers will turn away.

11.5 Google ads for money making

If someone has their website and blog interest, then they can easily make money through it. If you want to start making money through your website, there are several ways to google ads, affiliate marketing, subscriptions, and many more.

So here we are discussing how we can earn through google ads. For making money through google ads, you first need a stunning website because good websites make you earn better. Advertising can provide a healthy way of earning using your blog and website. First of all, we need to worry about those specific types of website which generate good revenue from google ads because the right steps lead to better results in Google AdSense. The most two important things which required for making money through your website are good content and a lot of traffic. To increase traffic on a particular website, one needs to optimize its search engine and social media platform. Mainly there is that kind of content that supports that take back the user on that particular website. The content should be real, so genuine visitors can be generated quickly and without making so many efforts.

Lets first, we discuss what the strategical plan of earning money through google ads for that we have to understand how these algorithm works are. So basically, ads are being created by the advertisers who want to promote their product, and they paid for showing their ads on a particular website. Now we understand what Google AdSense is, the answer to this question is that AdSense works on the matching phenomenon as they match ads to your website based on the content which is provided by your website. For that, publishers get enough money according to their quality of content. Here one more thing to understand that the advertiser needs not to pay the same amount for the different ads. The price may or may not be different for each ad.

There are mainly three steps for getting paid by AdSense

1. Space should be available

People make their website according to the area and hosting they buy online, so it is essential to make sure there should be space for pasting the code for ads. Wherever you want to place your ads, you need to make space over there.

2. The extreme highest paying ads

The highest paying ads should be shown on your website for earning a handsome amount from the ads.

3. Your payment gets done

Then, finally, the processing of billings from the respective advertisers and the network issues are handled then it's the final step in getting money in your account.

Here, one more interesting fact about AdSense is that we can't put the ads on our website according to our choice. Google searching algorithms make sure, and they provide us better suitable ads according to their own decisions. It is an automatic procedure in which google ads target our website's content according to their intelligent algorithms.

Types of AdSense for making money

There are several ads google can place on our website. Some of them are listed below:

- **Graphic ads:** Basically, graphics ads are the image type of advertisements that are shown on any website. These ads come up with a variety of sizes.
- **Interactive ads:** These types of ads include animation, including HTML technology and even, can use video and flash too.
- **Text:** In this category of ads, only text is shown on the web page, with several different sizes and fonts changing their colors.
- **Animated Images:** Different animated images are shown on the screen concerning changing their size and color of the picture.

Payment through Google AdSense

The payment method of google AdSense works on the threshold value, which is fixed for every website that is $100. here threshold means you have to earn $100 every month to make sure to deposit money in your bank and for the cheque. For any reason, if you are not able to earn $100, it rolls back and adds a payment method on the next month.

Guidelines for making money through Google AdSense
First of all, if we want to generate the right amount of money from our particular website or blog without taking any yield that its new account or old account, then we must need a plan. Which plan includes how to do work step by step according to google terms and policy to get better earn. Here are some of the steps that are mentioned:

- **Webmaster policies:** The webmaster and sitemap should comply with the Google rules and adhere to all other regulations and ads by google to putting ads on your particular website.
- **Don't click on your own websites' ads:** Always try to generate genuine visitors on your website; otherwise, google has the right to stop your website ads.

- **Content should be up to mark:** Content should possess a good level, so readers may take an interest in reading your blog and website. As we already discussed that excellent content should lead to earning an excellent handsome amount of money.

- **Organic traffic:** Organic traffic means the visitors who visit our website are genuine. If you want to get free organic traffic, then search engine optimization and article writing marketing can undoubtedly boost you.

- **Mobile version of the website:** It is necessary to make a mobile version of the blog and webpages because most people carry it on mobile if we compare it with the desktop or personal computers. It is easy to access and easy to handle. That is why it is required to have a mobile version of the website and blog.

So, we can conclude that AdSense is a suitable monetization method, but taking some consideration into mind is genuine visitors and organic traffic on your blog and website. Besides Google AdSense, there are some more techniques that can be sued to generate money through these technical website making skills. For example, affiliate marketing, coaching your blog, consulting, etc.

 Note: Only rich content can take you to income in 6 digits from just google AdSense.